A
FLAT
PLACE

A FLAT PLACE

moving through

empty landscapes,

naming complex trauma

NOREEN MASUD

MELVILLE HOUSE
BROOKLYN · LONDON

A Flat Place: Moving Through Empty Landscapes, Naming Complex Trauma

First published in 2023 by Melville House
Copyright © Noreen Masud, 2022
All rights reserved
First Melville House Printing: April 2023

Melville House Publishing
46 John Street
Brooklyn, NY 11201
and
Melville House UK
Suite 2000
16/18 Woodford Road
London E7 0HA

mhpbooks.com
@melvillehouse

ISBN: 978-1-68589-024-7
ISBN: 978-1-68589-025-4 (eBook)

Library of Congress Control Number 2023931177

Designed by Patrice Sheridan

Printed in the United States of America
1 3 5 7 9 10 8 6 4 2

A catalog record for this book is available from the Library of Congress for my friends

To say, as some do, that the self *must* be narrated, that only the narrated self can be intelligible and survive, is to say that we cannot survive with an unconscious.

Judith Butler, *Giving an Account of Oneself*

Contents

Introduction

Every morning in Lahore, as we drove to school, there came a point when I'd quieten and coil into myself. Jammed together with me in the back seat, my sisters went on quarrelling, poking one another with elbows, voices raised in jeers or protest. But I stared out of the window, holding myself taut as we passed the carpet seller, his rugs spread over the grass embankment on the side of the road and pinned up on the trees with long nails. My favourite moment of the day was coming, and I had to be ready.

If I wasn't prepared—if a kick broke my concentration, or wrestling siblings knocked my head out of its line of sight—I'd miss the miracle. Because when we reached the end of that cramped road, our car dodging donkey carts and street sellers and dashing children, and turned the corner—in that instant, the world opened out. Lahore vanished around me. All I could see, stretching out for miles, were huge empty fields.

We'd crossed from city into fairy tale. And, every morning, no one noticed but me.

I've forgotten so much of my early life, but those fields have stayed with me. How could there be so much empty land in the middle of crowded, parched, shouting Lahore? How could anything be so deeply, achingly green? I felt that green on my skin and in my dry throat. The school playground never kept its grass more than a few days. Every year it was resown, optimistically, the seeds sending up dark dusty tufts, as though Lahore might decide to change its climate. But within days the ground had baked solid and brown under the blasting sun and the thousands of small feet in shiny black shoes.

Not those fields. Through summer sun, monsoon downpour and winter mists, and through the spring whose creeping heat I experienced like the sound of a distant, sinister drum, they stayed lush. I kept my stare fixed on that beautiful alien colour as the trees flicked past the window: a long row of trunks, lining the road, which measured out my journey to school as rhythmically as a heartbeat.

The fields were perfectly, shimmeringly flat. No people crossed them. No hills, no valleys, no machinery. There was nothing for the eye to light upon. Good, I thought. My gaze didn't want to be distracted. It wanted to fly and fly, like a bird skimming the grass, without stopping. I imagined picking up every inch of ground and storing that expanse inside me for when I needed it. Later—standing on the edge of the school playground, watching the flies cluster by my feet, or staring blankly at my teacher's face in the classroom—I could take myself back to the fields, and live there in the cool quiet by myself.

Everything in my Lahore was cramped. Five of us shared a bedroom, four of us shared the back seat. So that expansive emptiness seemed impossible: like a glimpse of the divine. I could send my eyes running off over the fields, even as I stayed jammed in the back seat of the car against my little sister Forget-Me-Not, my hands up against the glass. ('Don't touch the glass,' my mother said, from the front seat. 'It leaves a smear that never comes off.') Running, in my mind, faster than was possible, stretching my muscles as hard as they could possibly be stretched. In that space, no matter how I moved—if I flung myself or rolled or cartwheeled (I didn't know how to cartwheel)—I knew I wouldn't come up against anything.

If I walked far enough, I thought, over those fields, out past the edges of my vision, soon the road and the car and my fighting sisters would vanish, and there would just be me. Standing in the middle of that flatness, turning slowly, with nothing to see on any side. Then, maybe, I could rest.

Near the end of my British grandmother's life, one memory came back to her again and again, as her appetite dwindled and she shrank into her chair.

'I'm with my friend Joy,' she said to me, smiling at the air, one autumn morning six weeks before she died. 'Oh, Joy. She was wonderful. It was the right name for her. Joy!'

'How old were you?' I was arranging five tiny pieces of dolly mixture on a plate at her elbow, hoping to tempt her.

'Perhaps about ten. I can just see her now. Walking up the hill in front of me.' Her smile caught and stayed. Half an hour later, she'd lost the memory of telling me and she described the scene again: watching Joy climb that hill, and climbing up after her.

I think that memory of walking after Joy lay at the core of who my grandmother was. To steal a phrase by Virginia Woolf, it was the base that her life stood upon.

Woolf considered her own life founded on an early memory, from when she was a child on holiday in St Ives, in Cornwall. She describes the scene in an autobiographical fragment from 'Sketch of the Past':

> If life has a base that it stands upon, if it is a bowl that one fills and fills and fills—then my bowl without a doubt stands upon this memory . . . It is of hearing the waves breaking, one, two, one, two, and sending a splash of water over the beach; and then breaking, one, two, one, two, behind a yellow blind. It is

of hearing the blind draw its little acorn across the floor as the wind blew the blind out. It is of lying and hearing this splash and seeing this light, and feeling, it is almost impossible that I should be here; of feeling the purest ecstasy I can conceive.

A base that life stands upon. Woolf connects everything she is to that simple early memory. What base does my life stand upon? When I read 'Sketch of the Past' as an undergraduate, I put down the book and knew, without doubt, that my life stands upon those flat, empty fields in Lahore.

Flat landscapes, I realized, had always given meaning to a world that made no sense to me. We grew up watching life through living-room windows which had been covered first with bars and then with a layer of chicken wire, just in case. My mother was British and bewildered; my father was Pakistani, and knew—he said—how things worked, and what was at stake. He made the rules, and it did not occur to my mother that they might be broken. No speaking to neighbours. No inviting classmates or friends round. And nice girls stayed at home, safe behind the chicken wire.

Usually my mother got on quietly with things, while chaos raged around us. At five every morning she rose to boil the huge silver *daigchees* of milk, so that by the time we woke up it would be safe and cool to drink. She killed cockroaches when they crawled out of drains; she ran downstairs when my grandmother hollered for her; she knelt every evening by the power outlet, burning pesticide mats to kill the mosquitoes. My mother thrives in a crisis, and every night in Pakistan was a small crisis. It wouldn't occur to her to complain. But the relentless noise of Lahore pierced even her stoicism. The car horns, pressed down and held with both hands. The shouting. The motorcycles revving. The sudden bangs that were usually firecrackers and not guns. Usually.

So every once in a while, my mother would break, would wander through the house, back and forth, crying out against the relentless noise. She had grown up in rural Scotland, a lonely child in a half-empty house, where you could hear one car coming for a mile and every creak sounded loud. The only life I knew was hot and dirty and crowded, bodies pressed against each other: oil sizzling, loud music on my grandmother's TV, my uncles arguing. Between fourteen and twenty-five people lived in my house in Lahore at any one time, coming and going. So did, at various times, rabbits, goats, chickens, geese, budgies, dogs, cats, turkeys, peacocks, chicks and parrots. My father had his own bedroom; the rest of us—my mother, my three sisters, and I—lived in another, piling over each other, shouting and fighting in hushed voices so as not to wake him while he slept. There was nowhere to run.

Things happened all at once, all the time. My grandfather, half mad, paced the corridors shouting 'Help!' The house caught fire. Furniture piled up and was covered with sheets, as if the chairs and sofas had died and were waiting to be laid out for burial. Our garden was a little bleached patch, too hot to step into in summer. At night mosquitoes arrived, buzzing malaria, and we hid inside. Armed robbers came to the house; we children sat in the bath and turned off all the lights and waited, holding our breath, as downstairs a man held a gun to my aunt's head.

Life bit hard, I knew. It was a fact one couldn't get around. The way things were. Everything was scary and dangerous and happening right in front of me. Reality meant living continuously up against a basic truth: that the world would hide nothing from you, even if you were eight years old.

Those fields on the way to school gave me a fantasy of space to stretch out in, and distance from the chaos at home. And yet they also seemed to sum up the way life was, when I was eight and starting to notice things. The world was a flat plain with nowhere to hide.

It was better to know, I thought, than to have teachers and friends pretend that everything was all right. Nothing was all right. I was a small hard creature, knowing what I knew, as resolute and still and enclosed in myself as the flat landscape that drew me towards it. I waited, every morning, as the dawn mists rose over Lahore, for the car to round the corner and open out onto those fields. And the flat fields told me, wordlessly, that I wasn't mad. That I knew something important. That they knew too, and would reflect it back to me, whenever I needed.

Flat landscapes have always given me a way to love myself.

I had no words for this feeling, in either English or Urdu. There was no space, in the house, in my family, in my head, to say them or struggle towards them. There was no space at all. So I said nothing, not to my uncle who drove us to school, leaning out of the window to yell the very worst words in Punjabi at other cars, nor to my parents or my sisters. Instead I stared silently at the electric blue signs in front of the fields. They promised a hospital, in Urdu, which I couldn't read quickly enough—my uncle liked to take the car up to a hundred miles an hour, to make us scream—and English, which I could.

The signs stood there for as long as I can remember, guarding those empty fields. As we grew, and the back seat of the car became more and more cramped, the signs began to flake and peel and buckle, until no one could read them at all. Nothing ever got built there. Or rather, I left Pakistan in a hurry, eight years later, long before any hospital sprang up.

————

I didn't think much about those fields again for years, until I took up a place on a master's course in Cambridge.

I'd never even visited Cambridge before. This didn't matter. It was part of my stance, at that time, that decisions ultimately meant nothing. It didn't matter how long you pored over them: you could stare at the surface of a problem from all angles, and still be none the wiser. So I glanced over my options and said yes to Cambridge and thought no more about it.

Still groggy from a hasty root canal performed that same morning, I wobbled south on the train from Scotland, staying overnight in the beautiful cathedral city of Ely with an old friend of my mother's. She drove me to Cambridge the next day, as the sun was rising. Halfway through the trip, I bolted upright and stared out of the window, her conversation fading in my ears. Sun cut through the haze on the flat sea of the fields, and as the pale brown tree trunks whipped past, I realized that I had been here, or a version of here, before. Without warning, I was back in Lahore.

I spent that year in Cambridge like a ghost, unable to think or feel. My stomach had always hurt, since I was a little girl, and no one could work out why. Now the pain grew so bad that I stopped eating for days at a time. I went to classes and said nothing, fumbling in my bag under the seminar table for painkillers and staring at the opposite wall. The wind which ran its blade down the flat land seemed to scrape away all colour. What I remember is bleached green and my feet in leather shoes, moving over the ground as if through a trance. I remember standing near the river Cam, staring at the pale fields, quivering under frost, and how my gaze looped over and over their flat surfaces, hypnotically. As though seeking something it could never find—and didn't want to find, even as it went on looking.

Something was wrong, I knew. Something was beating its wings at the edge of my memory, trying to get in, like a bird hitting a window. But whenever I tried to look straight at that thought, that feeling, all I saw in my mind was an image of the flat fields of Lahore, stretching as far as I could see, with nothing particular to focus on. It was as though I was trying to remember something which didn't exist. I searched the landscape for a clue, anything at all to guide me, and came up with nothing. And yet the image of that bare space held me tight in its grip.

From the outside I seemed fine. I went to classes and wrote my dissertation and did my laundry. We studied W. G. Sebald's *The Rings of Saturn*, a book about haunting and memory. Our tutor took us on a field trip to Orford Ness, one of the landscapes that Sebald describes in his book: a spit of shingle in Suffolk. It was very quiet and very flat. Pebbles crunched underfoot, and on the bare horizon the bodies of lost things stuck up out of the land. Abandoned military buildings, rusted and flaking. Twisted metal remnants. Orford Ness had been used for aborted army experiments for many years in the twentieth century, grand projects started and cut short before they came to fruition. A few birds walked on long legs around these dead monuments. The place could have been drawn straight out of a post-apocalyptic film, levelled as though by some catastrophe.

But I didn't need the rusting military towers or the snapped-off bases of the radio masts to be thrilled by Orford Ness. What fascinated me was its flatness. Gazing across the shingle, I felt how little the landscape needed me. It was indifferent. I could have been a tuft of thistledown, blown harmlessly over the flat expanse, leaving no trace. Displaying everything on a single plane, Orford Ness gave up everything it had to offer, immediately—as though it had no fear of my judgement. No need to seduce me with deferred promises, of a new delight just round the next bend, of a peak to be scaled, or crevasse to be explored. This was a landscape absorbed, purely, in being itself.

The other students asked intelligent questions and made searching, thoughtful remarks about Sebald, but I stayed silent. I was held captive by this unyielding, silent space, and I began to understand two things. That flatness wasn't an absence—not in the way we might assume it is—but something strong and original and living. And that you could fall in love with flatness, gazing at it forever.

'The thing is,' I said to the therapist, 'nothing *that* awful ever happened to me.'

Eight years had passed since Orford Ness, and fifteen since Pakistan. I was thirty now, mostly made of bones, and things—I had finally admitted—were bad. I tucked myself into the corner of the too-big chair and stared at the waste paper basket.

'Not really. Not compared to what happens to some people in Pakistan. I'm a girl with an education. That makes me one of the very, very luckiest people. And everything is okay now, I have a great life. But I just feel so desperate. Like we're actually all walking through a wasteland, and no one can see it except me. And I can't stop thinking about Pakistan, and I don't even know why, because there's nothing really to think about.'

My therapist screwed up her face, sympathetically.

'That's the way with complex trauma,' she said. 'It's more than one event, or even several. It's like this tinge of horror that suffuses everything.'

The first time the therapist had mentioned complex trauma, I'd stared blankly at her. She was exaggerating, I thought. Trauma derived from properly horrifying experiences, like a war or a terrible attack, and involved flashbacks to the event. How could I be traumatized when there was no event to flash back to? There was nothing I could point to and say: this is what happened to me, this is why I'm the way I am. Nothing to explain the paralysing horror I had always forced myself through, the war zone I saw in the world when other people seemed to see beauty. When I looked back at my childhood, it was impossible to pick out any particular act of violence or fear which stood out as exceptional, as the root of it all. So why did my life in Pakistan continue to grip me so tightly—a smear on my mind which would never come off?

But I'd begun, slowly, to understand that complex post-traumatic stress disorder, or cPTSD, was different. It was particularly difficult to treat, because—like a flat landscape—it didn't offer a significant landmark, an event, that you could focus on and work with. Complex post-traumatic stress, according to the psychiatrist Judith Lewis Herman, is the result of 'prolonged, repeated trauma,' rather than individual traumatic events. It's what happens when you're born into a world, shaped by a world, where there's no safety, ever. When the people who should take care of you are, instead, scary and unreliable, and when you live years and years without the belief that escape is possible.

When you come from a world like this, when all your muscles are trained to tension and suspicion, normal life feels unbearable. It doesn't make sense, getting up, going to class, eating lunch, returning home, sleeping. You don't trust it. It doesn't feel real. And unreality can hurt more than pain.

So I lived my life in Britain, the one that was supposed to be better—my happy ending, away from my father and that house in Pakistan—feeling as though I was on fire, and I couldn't explain why. I walked around in the world and held a neutral look on my face, all the time, while something inside cried and cried. My body didn't seem to work properly: I was always tired. Seeing other people, even people I loved, made me panic and vanish inside myself. And I couldn't seem to feel enough. I couldn't desire things, desire others, in the way they were offered to me, while everyone around me was falling in and out of love.

Worse, when I tried to describe what I felt, people seemed baffled, or scared.

'But it's okay! You're here now!'

'But isn't that just what life is like in Pakistan?'

And I could only retreat into silence, because I couldn't explain it.

'It's all right that you feel this way,' my therapist said gently. 'Things were unsafe, all the time. And no one could help you.'

My father died in August 2019, a month after I turned thirty. I was at a wedding, still chatting to my friend as I picked up my phone and read my sister's text:

Aba had a heart attack this morning and died.

I showed the text to everyone at the table, including the people I didn't know, then laughed at their horrified faces and got up and walked outside. It was raining faintly, and my feet grew wet and slipped around inside their red summer sandals.

There was no question of attending the funeral, even if I had been welcome. My Pakistani passport had expired. Instead, I tracked down footage of it on Facebook. My father was buried within twenty-four hours, amidst rain and shouting mourners grappling over his body in monsoon mud. I saved photos of that body, grey and bruised, to look at later. So that I would know where he was.

For the first months after he died I couldn't bear the thought that he was in the earth. Not that I felt sad for him. His death seemed appropriate, and perhaps overdue. But if I had been able to put him aside in life, in death he suddenly existed very physically in the world. The ground had swallowed him up, but he was still there, all bones and eyes and muscle, newly made into an object which wouldn't go away.

So I did what comforts me: some research. How quickly he rotted, I discovered, would depend on the manner of his burial, the pH and dampness of the soil, the ambient temperature, the depth of the grave, whether he was wrapped in cloths. I scrutinized the photos, trying to work these things out. I didn't feel confident in what I concluded. I made a chart of possible options for his decay. There were too many. I hid the chart under a pile of papers.

Through my academic networks, I tracked down and emailed a forensic pathologist, apologetically. The pathologist was kind, but she confirmed my fears: it could be anything up to—what? Nine months? A year?—before all that was left were his bones and I could bring my gaze back up from the depths of the soil to the tranquil flat surface, a world without him, now, on it.

Why do I love flat landscapes so much? Why do they quieten the thing in me that's always crying? Flatness is a puzzling thing to love. Ever since the Romantic poets tramped around Europe, rhapsodizing over the magnificence of dramatic landscapes, it has been mountains—not flatlands—which have been considered beautiful, breathtaking, valuable. Mont Blanc was a particular favourite in the nineteenth century, thrusting upwards into the poetry of Percy Shelley and Samuel Taylor Coleridge. The iconic Romantic painting *Wanderer Above the Sea of Fog* (1818), by Caspar David Friedrich, places mountains swirling with mists at centre stage. Mountains shape our emotions into surges of joy, plunges of passion; we come away feeling emotionally refreshed.

They've also come to symbolize human power, ambition, success. The very sight of a mountain, offering a summit to reach, pushes one to exceed oneself, to drive beyond one's limitations. How coercive that is. How cruel, to instil the belief that one must always be striving. People climb Everest, they tell us, because it is there. Pakistan is proud of its K2, perhaps the most dangerous mountain in the world: for every four climbers who reach the summit, a fifth dies. In Pakistan, these stories are told with a hint of relish. On mountains—as in stories—tragedy is what counts. The country fought hard to keep territorial control over the Karakoram Mountains, shoving back against India and China for its share of the shaggy range which borders the Himalayas. In 1999, when I was ten, India and Pakistan fought the Kargil War, high up in the mountains, and thousands of people died. As with so many deaths in Pakistani history, no one seems quite sure—or perhaps wants to know—exactly how many. A big number, though. Mountains are the all-important stage for personal and national achievement: summits reached, blood spilled.

If mountains are poetry, flatlands are prose: cookbooks or technical manuals, practical but dull. You can build towns on flat land, construct railways on it, plant crops for food, walk easily across its level surface. Flatness enables the boring business of living—but it's hard to imagine anything really exciting happening there. So how do we make stories about flat landscapes? Is there anything at all to say about a space in which nothing important seems to happen?

And if not—why do I want, endlessly, to look at and talk about them?

When we stand in a flat landscape, we find ourselves in a kind of contradiction. Everything there is to see lies freely open to us. And yet there seems to be nothing to see. We don't know how to organize this space in our minds. How to look at it. We stand scanning, right and left, but there's nothing to fix our eyes on. We are used to 'reading' landscapes: moving through a distinct foreground and midground and background. Small, human details in the front; big shadows of relief in the back. But faced with a flat landscape, uniform as far as the eye can see, we struggle. It's as though the landscape is sending us a message that we're unable to decipher.

And yet we can't always just pass them by. Underneath all the noisy love songs to mountains, there's a quiet tradition of writers and artists lingering in flat landscapes. L. S. Lowry infuriated local councillors by painting a flat seascape for Salford City Council in 1952, where the bare surface of the sea offers no visual interest. There is a rich line of literary accounts of crossing the wide bare sandflats of Morecambe Bay, where the horizon tricks the eye into disregarding the tide's swift motion, the patches of treacherous quicksand. And the flat landscapes of Orkney hold space open for extraordinary wide skies, inspiring a tradition of uncanny myths and legends, recording the sensation of things lurking just under the surface of our everyday experience. Things which we can never fully know.

I think this is the heart of it. Flat landscapes ask us to tolerate not knowing things. Not knowing what is beneath the surface, whether anything is. A flat landscape's combination of complete exposure and complete withholding asks us to accept that there are things we'll never understand.

But they also—I hope—leave hints about how we might live in their space of uncertainty. Since Freud, modern psychology has loved the concrete event: the idea that if we are depressed or disturbed, it's because something specific happened, long ago. A landmark in our lives, a turning point, the moment of trauma. Those memories might be repressed but can and must be fished out eventually. But not all lives are shaped by the definite peaks of event. Some lives seem utterly flat and undramatic, and yet something electric runs over their surface, holding the gaze. Some lives like my own.

A flat place helps us to reimagine what it means for something to 'happen' and to rethink what it means for something to 'matter.' To accept that not all discoveries involve digging for answers, or ascending heights—that sometimes it's just a case of staying, quietly and steadily, with what you already know, and have always known.

In particular, they provide solace for someone who doesn't experience conventionally heightened feeling. In a world where exaggerated expressions of emotion are the norm, on social media and in the workplace's stringent emotional labour demands, the quiet presence of a flat landscape—refusing to rise into anything —gives me permission to be numb, to be without feeling or desire.

I never once set foot in those fields on the outskirts of Lahore. I only ever stared at them through a smudged car window. But I spend my life in that flat landscape. When sounds drown me in a crowded room, when I find myself face to face with a person who locks eyes with mine as they talk, when I struggle to make myself understood in conversation—then I'm back there, standing in a field which stretches away on every side, the mists descending.

Love, I learned with my therapist, involves feeling 'seen': feeling our sense of ourselves mirrored and validated by the other. With their clear stark lines and whistling winds, the flat landscapes that shaped my childhood seem to mirror the sensations of intensity, blankness and self-sufficiency that have kept me going through my life, even as safety, sexual passion and emotional intimacy never showed up for me. Did these feelings have to be a consolation prize, a poor substitute for human connection? Or might they somehow be a bridge—a way into loving contact with other people?

'Nothing can happen until you feel safe,' my therapist said, gently. 'Relational trauma takes a really, really long time to repair. It makes complete sense to me that you connect most to objects, when people have been so threatening to you.'

She watched me. I watched the wall.

If I wanted to learn to rest in the wider world—the world which feels spiky and strange, which hurts like a carpet burn and forces me into feeling—I had to learn to share what doesn't want to be shared, what vanishes when I dig the bones up and drag them into the light. To trust that the thoughts and the traumatized memories which translate, for me, into flat landscapes might exist as more than a private, unreachable image. So I began a series of journeys across landscapes which I felt—however absurdly—were somehow attuned to me and might somehow offer answers: a language which honours, instead of denying, my love of numbed, inanimate things. My flat feelings, my memories of a flat life.

A FLAT PLACE

CHAPTER 1

The First Flat Place

'I see a ring,' said Bernard, 'hanging above me. It quivers
and hangs in a loop of light.'
'I see a slab of pale yellow,' said Susan, 'spreading away until
it meets a purple stripe.'
'I hear a sound,' said Rhoda, 'cheep, chirp; cheep, chirp;
going up and down.'
'I see a globe,' said Neville, 'hanging down in a drop against
the enormous flanks of some hill.'
'I see a crimson tassel,' said Jinny, 'twisted with gold threads.'
'I hear something stamping,' said Louis. 'A great beast's foot
is chained. It stamps, and stamps, and stamps.'
—Virginia Woolf, *The Waves*

From Pakistan, two flat landscapes stay with me. One outside our
house, one inside it.

Outside: the green misted fields glimpsed from the car window,
stretching out wide and far away, on my way to school.

And inside: the flat stone floors of the house. I can still feel
them against my cheek, under my hands. Caramel-coloured marble
blocks, each just under a metre square. They were embedded with
grey and white and pale blue pebbles, and sheared perfectly smooth:
joined together with dark grey frosted glass. In the heat of the day,

every day, I lay on that cold floor, moving my hands over it slowly, in small circles and in large ones.

When I stare at any flat landscape now, I get the same feeling of coolness: in my throat, in my hands, and at the back of my neck. My gaze loops over and over the stark surface. It feels like rubbing my hands over a smooth table, or a cold sheet of ice. But very few things in nature are truly, perfectly flat. As my eye roves, I know I'm seeking something. Will there be a flaw, a knot, a gnarl, to break the surface? Half of me hopes I'll never find one. Half of me goes on searching, uneasily.

Something went wrong in my life, years ago. A knot or a gnarl, embedded somewhere, which must have sent everything strange. But I can't seem to find it.

The memory theorist Douwe Draaisma argues that we only remember things which are aberrations from the normal. I can't remember what happened to me because it was the substance of my normal. But one of my clearest memories is of lying on that stone floor. Ants crawled across it, just as lizards crawled up the walls and cockroaches roamed the bathroom and frogs sheltered in the kitchen cupboards. I put my hands flat on the ground, index fingers and thumbs forming the shape of an ace of spades, trapping an ant. It blundered around this new wall, trying to find a way out, until eventually it gave up and climbed up onto my hand. I lifted my hand and watched the ant crawling down my arm, round and round. My hair prickles at the memory of it biting, again and again.

It's important to say that my life in Pakistan was unusual. It was an odd life compared to British lives, but for Pakistan, too, it was an unusual life. My father put his two big hands on the ground around us, and we crawled around inside. If I remember the floor more clearly than anything, it's because for thirteen years that was my world. The cold marble; the fluorescent lights; the dusty smell of the chicken wire over the windows. In the summers, when there was no school, months could go past without us leaving the two rooms on the upper floor of our house. My mother, my three sisters, and me: Rabbit, Spot and Forget-Me-Not. Those aren't their real names, but I think you could have guessed that.

No one else I knew lived like this. Many, many Muslim and Pakistani women have rich, juicy, vital lives, integrated with other people, fulfilling their ambitions. But also, many don't, because Pakistani society lets things go both ways. In particular, it turns a blind eye to anything that happens between fathers and daughters.

My father was a doctor, and the eldest son in his family: in charge at work and at home. He specialized in diabetes, which afflicts nearly a fifth of the Pakistani population. By all accounts he did it very, very well. 'Oh, you're Dr Anwar's daughter!' my teachers would exclaim. I squirmed. His intelligence was impatient, fitful, indifferent to rules; he skirted and tore through the tedious twists of bureaucracy which colonization had left hanging round our country like cobwebs. He became known as a genius, a maverick, doing what he thought best and never asking for permission, in the way that men are allowed to do all over the world. Anyone who disagreed with him, he thought, was stupid and ignorant. And he had a specific disdain for Pakistan: what he saw as its inefficiency, slowness, superstition.

'I don't worship Allah,' he used to say, smiling. 'I worship my god, Apollo.'

My father was an Anglophile who despised most other Pakistanis. It became part of his mythology. 'Dr Anwar is so rude,' his patients would say lovingly, 'but such a great man.' He wore very fine Western suits, and leather shoes which he would have me fetch and polish and slide on to his feet. He shaved his beard and trimmed his moustache; he took the top off a water cooler and used it to brew illegal cider in our bathtub. He made us taste the results. The alcohol ran warm down my throat and pooled in my stomach.

The great man was a megalomaniac and a fantasist. He'd done work for the president, he told us. For the army. When you're as good as I am, he said, you can do whatever you want. And ironically, despite my father's Westernization, only Pakistan would handle him deferentially enough for his tastes. Only its glitching, dropping rhythms—lurching from crisis to crisis—would let him dodge through the system without answering to anybody.

Other people don't understand, my father told us. Stay away from them. He loathed the weddings, the visits, the community relationships that formed the glue of Pakistani society. If we spoke to the neighbours, or went to our friends' houses, they'd only start asking for favours and taking up his time. So that wasn't allowed.

To his credit, he never complained about having four girls and no boys. 'My girls are my boys,' he used to tell people who hinted delicately at our family's tragedy. We would be every bit as good, he decided. We'd be doctors and engineers and mathematicians. Our hair was cut short, straight across our heads, and we were kept away from other children. Instead, shut inside, we were tested. Maths. Physics. Lateral thinking. And more abstract things: Can you identify your sisters by the scent of their pillows? Can you solve this riddle? If I put you up high, so high that you freeze with fear, can you work out how to climb down?

I always failed.

He was determined to optimize us, mentally and physically. My medical records start at the age of sixteen, when I moved to the UK and registered with a doctor for the first time. Until then, my father did everything, as my mother held us, or held us down. It was all part of competing with the imaginary boys.

I don't know what all those injections were, throughout my childhood. They usually happened quite unexpectedly: my father arriving home, with a briefcase of vials and needles, ordering my mother to get us ready as he filled the syringes. Nor can I explain the heaps of tablets arranged next to my plastic mug of buffalo milk at breakfast and dinner. I never asked. I can't remember if I even thought of asking. Questions didn't tend to end in answers.

But I do know—because my father bragged about it, often— that there was nothing he couldn't get hold of, if he wanted. All he had to do, he told us, was pick up the phone. And I know that when my father decided that my little sister, Forget-Me-Not, was too short, he simply began injecting her with growth hormone.

I remember Forget-Me-Not, aged perhaps ten, standing in the middle of the living room, staring at nothing with her mouth slightly open, while my father hunched over her arm. I looked away, then let my mind spread and flatten. I began to go to a place where everything was present and nothing was knowable, and the sky arched high above us all.

Downstairs lived my grandparents, my aunts and uncles, and my cousins. It was an ordinary Pakistani set up on the face of it: a household of extended family, growing and growing as children brought home their wives and husbands, and had children of their own. In our family, though, there was none of the warmth and fun and intimacy that can make those households work. Everyone was frozen.

My grandmother was from Kashmir. She was ten when India and Pakistan were roughly and incompetently partitioned by a British man who'd never visited the subcontinent before. Cyril Radcliffe spent five weeks drawing lines across British India, and then he destroyed all his papers and left, glad to be shot of the heat and humidity. Chaos bloomed behind him. People from both sides fled across the border; as many as two million people were murdered in bouts of violence and ethnic cleansing. And the worst of it happened in Kashmir.

After six years growing up in the thick of the violence, my grandmother was married off at sixteen to a man who hardly spoke, and by seventeen she had my father. None of this was ever talked about. I pieced it together much later, after we'd left the country.

'If you hug a baby,' she said to me once, when she found me weeping over a dead chick whom I'd loved, 'it grows up weak. I didn't hug my children, and look how strong they are.'

Throughout my childhood, my grandmother sat on the right side of her green bed: cross-legged in the daytime, draped on her side in the evening. She talked and talked in Urdu, a language I never learned properly, and shouted, and supervised the food, which was brought to her in metal dishes for judgement. I understood enough of what she said at first—children only need small words—but by the time I was a teenager, our shared world had become complicated enough that we lacked the common language to describe it. Her hair was white. In the bottom of her wardrobe I found rose-scented talcum powder, in a red tin, and I poured it over my head to make my own hair white, until I choked on dusty roses.

I know almost nothing about my paternal grandfather, even though I was born in his house and lived with him for thirteen years. I have his mother's eyes. They shone out of a black-and-white photograph of her mounted in the hallway, an ornate dupatta over her head. My grandfather's skin was dark where my grandmother's was fair. He was a prison officer, and retired when I was about four: the prison marked the occasion with a gold-coloured plate, bigger than my head. He brought it home: I held it in both hands and stared at it. Sometimes he went off to the countryside, where he owned a small farm, and he lay on a rope bed in the sunshine for hours. Mostly, he shuffled up and down the corridors of our house dressed in a filthy dhoti, staring into the middle distance, dipping in and out of madness every few years. I only remember him speaking to me once. I was swinging a basket in my hand; he told me to stop. I stopped.

My grandfather had a heart attack when I was eleven. My father dealt with that like he dealt with everything. He spread a sheet over the dining-room table, laid him out, and operated, my grandfather blinking drowsily under local anaesthetic. When all that remained was to remove excess tissue from the incision, he ordered us all downstairs to witness him working. The wound was like a placenta, big and solid and fleshy. My father ran the points of needles under it, injecting anaesthetic all around. Dark fluid began to run in broad tracks down my grandfather's chest: either iodine or blood.

Rabbit and Spot, the twins—aged thirteen—had to help with the operation. I only had to watch, and to hold out a white dinner plate from our kitchen to receive the cut ribbons of my grandfather's meat. But when my father picked up the scalpel, I shut my eyes. He could force me to be there, but he couldn't make me be present.

I have one more memory which I connect with my grandfather.

I remember standing at the top of the marble stairs. The lights downstairs are out, but I can see the white sheets stretched over the furniture, and the chairs stacked up. Around them paces a tall man, with the head of a monkey and sightless black holes for eyes. He is wearing my grandfather's dhoti.

I stay very quiet, because it's essential that I am not seen.

This memory is not one that I can explain.

'It might have been real,' my mother says doubtfully. 'Someone had a monkey mask at some point, I think.'

'Do you think it's important,' a friend asks delicately, not wanting to say what is obvious, 'that he was wearing your grandfather's clothes?'

It is not interesting to me to ask if this image is my mind's code for something. Asking that question, digging down to reach my grandfather and pulling him out like a hair, would not tell me anything I don't already know.

The monkey paces between the shrouded sofas, in the darkness, while I watch from above.

Some stories make less sense the more you remember.

Outside the living-room window was a big empty lot, where rubbish piled up and dusty weeds grew. Sometimes I could see a stray dog rummaging, or a thin cat moving purposefully past with its tail held high. Every so often the lot would fill up, for a minute or so, with sheep and goats as a boy herded them through, often with a couple of oxen lumbering behind, or even—near Eid-ul-Azha—a camel. Though the main road ran straight past our house—a cacophony of beeping, shouting, zooming—if you focused hard on the empty lot, you could tune in to the quality of silence there, broken only by a creaking bicycle or an ice-cream vendor pedalling along. You could also see the neighbours' children, playing in their garden or in the street, or walking to the corner shop to buy fruity wafer biscuits, chilli jelly sweets, tamarind crisps.

We weren't allowed to talk to them, but I knew what they said about us, in the playground and in the parlours. 'Oh, him? The doctor? Well, you know what he did? He married a *gori* and now he keeps them all locked up in the house. All four daughters. They don't go anywhere.'

I ran my fingernails over the chicken wire, listening to them tap and rattle on the metal, back and forth, again and again, until my teeth hurt. It drove my father crazy, this fiddling.

Up on the left, crows nested against the window. They came back year after year, filling and refilling the same nest with chicks. Pressed up close to the glass, the birds turned into silhouettes. It was hard to make out much through the chicken wire, but you knew when the shadow landing at the nest was one of the parents, because little mouths suddenly gaped up in thick Y shapes, cheeping. When a shadow landed by the nest and the cheeping turned to screaming, you knew it was a mynah bird, come to scoop the chicks out of the nest and eat them.

When this happened, and if he was there, my father would fling himself out of his chair, bound across the room and bang on the window. I flinched when he did this; I always flinched when he moved quickly. But there was a sweetness, I thought even then, in that violent sentimentality. Such a huge, frightening man, caring passionately about three or four squashy baby birds.

We watched crows grow up and leave and new crows move in.

So I had that nest, and my mother and my sisters, and, peripherally, my extended family downstairs, and occasionally my father, erupting with rage or with a kind of precarious, dangerous warmth, as the mood took him. Apart from that, my world was made entirely of objects: the inert silent things with which I began my lifelong love affair.

The carpet downstairs had a broad, dark red border surrounding a beige middle section, curled all over with a pattern of paisleys. It was probably quite garish, but I was entranced. I didn't know the word 'paisley.' I called the shapes turnips. I spent hours walking over that carpet by myself, turning my feet to fit into every paisley, step by step.

The velour of the sofas, green and pink, was pale and shiny when it lay one way, dark and soft when it lay the other. I rucked my hands through it, rubbing it all up to deep colour, smoothing it all down. Making lines and patterns and wiping them off.

The lamp in the bedroom: pink turned to brown with dust, with tassels that made me sneeze. I ran my finger through the tassels, again and again.

A green pedestal fan turned slowly back and forth to stir air in the dining room. Once, when I was five, I reached out to stroke its metal grille. Immediately the world distorted, my whole body poisoned with metal spirals—and then it was over and I was standing by the fan, staring helplessly at it. It had bitten me.

I touched it again to see if I had imagined it. The same thing happened, worse this time.

I went to my mother, shaking, accusing the fan. I couldn't explain what it had done because I had no words for it. She took up a metal fork and walked over to it, and she touched the fork to the grille, with me clinging to her in terror. And the electric current from the broken, live machine travelled through us both.

When there is no novelty in your world, you become used to taking a long time to do one thing. Reading and rereading and rereading. But also: spending time with things which do nothing, which give you nothing. There is something which emerges in the space between you and the obdurate object. There is something which happens when your attention is not attracted, steered, managed; when you open yourself to something already fully exposed, with nothing more to know.

I learned very quickly that my cramped little life made me powerful in one horrible way. It stopped me from learning Urdu. This should have been impossible. I was born in Pakistan, to a Pakistani father. I lived there for sixteen years, thirteen of those in a household full of Urdu speakers. And yet, by the end of that time, I could hardly hold a conversation.

We went to school—where speaking English was strictly enforced, as is common in Pakistani schools—and we went home. Whenever we set foot outside—say, to walk from car to supermarket—men's heads would swivel. They stared at us right down the streets. This is partly because we were women, and partly because our mother was white. She'd met my father in the UK.

'We used to go for walks together,' she remembered, when I asked her why she'd married him. 'And once, he brought me a bunch of carnations.'

So my mother changed her name to Fatima, converted officially to Islam, and moved to Pakistan: to the rooms where she'd spend the next thirteen years.

When you keep four children locked up with their British mother—when you discourage them from spending time even with their own aunts and uncles and grandparents, who speak Urdu and Punjabi—when you send them to a school where children are punished for speaking anything but English, and ban them from visiting friends, or speaking to the neighbours—you'll find yourself with four children with perfect English and perfect English accents.

It surprised my father, and pleased him, and made him furious. His children would be winners, because the future was English. It was fifty years after Independence: English was still an official language of Pakistan, and an English accent a sign of education and prestige. People would sit up in attentive respect whenever his children spoke. But where did that leave him, with his Pakistani accent?

'Couldn't you speak Urdu to the children?' my mother asked.

'It's better to spend the time practising my English,' my father said stiffly. 'They're children. They'll pick up Urdu from the people around them.'

Through the barred windows, we peered out at the people around us.

My father practised on us, as he'd decided, perfecting his English over time. There were only one or two exceptions. Like the word 'donkey.' 'Monkey' was pronounced mun-kee, so, logically, 'donkey' was too. Monkeys and dunkeys. I bit my lip to stop myself laughing.

Once my father called me to him and told me to bring him a wet tissue. The screen of his computer was dirty.

I soaked a tissue carefully in water and brought it to him. He wiped at the screen, but the tissue fell apart.

'A bigger one!' He was annoyed.

I went back to the bathroom. I was scared already. I pulled a long length of tissue from the roll, counting in seconds, winding it round and round my hand. I carried the huge wad dripping back.

He took it from me, looked at it, then flung it to the floor at my feet. I focused hard on not jumping away.

Something in my father was shuddering. The machinery wasn't lining up; the cogs were biting and biting at the edges of a language they couldn't quite grasp. He couldn't find the word, and he could see me seeing him failing to find the word. He could see me knowing it wasn't my fault.

'A cloth,' he managed finally. 'Bring a wet cloth.'

My stone body went and dampened a small towel and brought it back to him.

'Wipe the screen.' He reclined in his chair. I leaned over him, barely breathing, as I ran the cloth round the four edges of the screen, over that old Windows 98 wallpaper of the lioness poised on a rock. Dabbing at running drops, attending to each corner.

'Now pick that up.' He waved his hand at the wet wad of tissue on the floor, already turning back to his work.

My father practised on us.

It felt like we were waiting for something to happen. Like anything was possible, however extreme. We waited for the sky to open and everything to fall down on us, all at once.

My father kept a gun in his glove compartment. When I asked him why he hid it, he was vague. He also kept one under his pillow. This would become an issue, later. One night he came home elated, with a brand-new pistol. We crowded around him to see. The thing about this gun was that it had a laser sight. This meant, my father explained, that you could be more precise about hitting your target. My mother turned and went into the bathroom, shutting the door that would not shut. It bounced and gaped open again.

He let us aim the laser on the walls, the wardrobe, each other.

A lot of the training he gave us was, at its root, about how to look gracious, or blank, when people aimed their laser sights upon you. In Pakistan you're always being watched, because there are so many bored and frustrated people. The only thing to do, if you're a stay-at-home wife—the only outlet for your rage and grief—is to talk about other people. My sister Spot once wore the same *shalwar kameez* two days running, and a week later my father stomped into the room with his eyes full of fire. Everyone had been talking about it; it had reached him in his clinic. The grapevines were rooted deep and wide. You couldn't trust anyone.

So my father tested how far he could push us until we reacted. He gathered us at the table and gave us long, abstract lessons, lasting hours. I don't know what they were about. But the point wasn't really to understand. The point was to stay absolutely still. If you moved or fidgeted you would be pulled off the chair and hit. I remember this happening. What I do not remember is whether it is me it is happening to. I seem to be both inside it, being hit myself, and outside it, facing the child who is being hit, as their feet slip on the floor under them, almost falling, held up by one arm and being struck by the other, while my mother watched. That was one test. Another was about privacy. We had to learn that we had no right to it. When I entered my teens, my father began to open my post in front of me. He'd tear open the envelope, looking not at it but at me. Watching me, to see if I would react.

He was always very careful. Nothing happened to us, really. When my father threw things at me—a pen, a book, a part of an air-conditioning unit—he always made sure that he missed.

This isn't an inspirational story. This isn't a story about keeping the flame of hope alive through adversity, and burning through to the other side, where what is wished for can at last be had. This is a story, I think, about what happens when in a very real sense that flame of hope is put out entirely. When forever after you can't find the muscle strength, deep in you, to rise to the moment when something wished-for might actually be attained, or even when something might be wished for in the first place.

There was no chance, in Pakistan, that things would get better. My dreams were very small. I wanted to do an O level in English Literature. Language tapped out a rhythm on the inside of my skull when I could hold nothing else in my head. Then—I hardly dared to look straight at the idea—I wanted to do an A level. After that, what was the best-case scenario? I could win financial aid to attend university abroad, majoring in biology or maths—and perhaps, if I was covert about it, minoring in literature. And then what? I would graduate and come home: a twenty-two-year-old girl from a culturally conservative Muslim family in Pakistan. I would work in something science-related for a few years, maybe, and then marry. Unlike the other girls at my school, my sisters and I weren't allowed to mix with boys, any boys at all, so the marriage would be arranged with one of my father's younger colleagues: someone clever but not too clever, a protégé whom he'd groomed to support him. And the person selected for me to marry would—this goes without saying—be a man. The easiest next step after that would be to die, because no part of what would have followed would have been survivable.

Childhood was the best it got, and childhood was already something to stay very still and breathe through. So when my chest started pushing itself up, and my armpits softened into fuzz, I was horrified. The sick feeling started settling deep into me. Adulthood was coming: the bleak future. At first I pretended it wasn't happening. Then I spent nights lying on my stomach, pushing down on one side of my chest with both hands. But the other kept on growing, and I couldn't push them both back in at once, and eventually I had breasts. I walked with my shoulders bent over slightly, to hide them. I pulled my dupatta round my whole chest, from neck to elbows.

Worse was to come. I woke up one morning, when I was fifteen, and God had gone. He'd always been a strange composite, formed of bits of Christian lore from my mother and Muslim uncertainties from school. But whatever He was, my personality had formed around

Him. He was like one of those oceanic creatures which collects hard bits of shell and rock and uses them to build a protective carapace. Now that small soft animal had died inside me, leaving its layers of calcium gathered around an empty centre.

I was very calm about it because there was no other choice. Apostasy is punishable by death in Islam. That's just the legal standpoint. I would legally have been executable in Pakistan for my loss of faith. My father and his laser-sighted gun. So I just needed to keep bending forwards slightly, around my breasts and now also around the hole where God had been.

When I was eight, we got a television in our living room. Unlike the one in my father's room, it couldn't get a signal for live TV, but we could watch video tapes on it. All the Disney films, pirated, in shiny cardboard sleeves, two tapes of *Button Moon* from the UK, and a documentary called *The Flight of the Condor*. We all loved the television, and we watched the cassettes over and over again, but for Forget-Me-Not it was a lifeline. She was too young to hide in a book like me and Rabbit and Spot, so she was often at a loss, before the television came. Forget-Me-Not would sit in front of the television, staring and rocking slightly, with her mouth open. That was how she watched. So it took several minutes, the first time, before I noticed she was responding even less than usual when I spoke.

'Forget-Me-Not?'

I shook her shoulder. She turned her face to me, large shocked eyes with nothing in them, vomit already beginning to dribble down her chin.

My mother appeared at my calls and swooped her through to the bedroom. Children throw up sometimes, and Forget-Me-Not threw up a lot. My older sisters watched while I dabbed at the vomit with a damp cloth. There wasn't much: only a few mouthfuls had come up. Dots on the rug. We thought nothing of it till we heard my mother's frightened shouts.

In the bedroom, my little sister was stripped and twitching on the bed. My mother held her with one hand and a towel in the other.

'She's having a seizure. Call your father. Call your father.'

My father's clinic was next to our house. When I ran to fetch him, he actually left his work and came up to the bedroom, which in itself made it feel like the world was ending. I preferred not to be near him, so I detached mentally from the scene, which means I don't remember what happened next. There was a lot of talking.

'It's a migraine,' my father said eventually.

My father suffered from migraines. He was sensitive to the strangest things: a single square of dark chocolate on his tongue could do it. Then he would lie in a dark room for hours, fans playing over him. Rabbit also got them. When she came home from school in a foul temper, you could see her eyelashes flutter in the sunlight that poured through the dusty windows.

None of what had happened to Forget-Me-Not looked like a migraine. The absence, the twitching limbs. But my father had spoken.

Later, as I grew older, I'd say to my mother, 'I think it could be epilepsy.' I said it over and over again. And my mother would make a humming noise, or change the subject, or say that migraines sometimes presented in very complex ways indeed.

We developed lots of words for the things that happened to Forget-Me-Not as she grew up. One of her episodes, we'd say. One of her funny turns. Never 'seizures.' And yes, we called them migraines, when she dropped to the ground in class and turned blue and wet herself. They didn't happen quite often enough to force the issue. But often enough that the feeling of living pressed up against something frightening and unknowable—that Forget-Me-Not both lived in that space and *was* that space—never went away.

Forget-Me-Not's moods swung. She smashed a glass door. She bit our cousin Mouse when she was angry. She stared, and twitched, vacant. Her feet turned in.

'Your father said it was migraines,' my mother said helplessly, years later. 'I did think it was something else. You don't get that jerking with migraine; he didn't see the first part, he came too late. But what could I have done?'

It is possible to know something you are not allowed to know. Very gently and deeply, like a whale passing beneath a boat, a long animal just under the surface.

Forget-Me-Not was eventually diagnosed at eighteen, once we had come to Britain, and once it was too late for many things. Her education, her friendships. Her memory was studded with holes where she'd been trapped in absence seizures—how many times a day, we don't know. That was the rocking and the twitching.

Now she wears tinted glasses in the supermarket where she works, to keep the light away. She bundles herself up in gloves and a hat, even in summer. But I can still see the drift beginning, many times a day, if the wind is blowing sharply across her ears, the stray into anger or incoherence which means something is or could be about to happen. And sometimes it happens and sometimes it doesn't. Sometimes it happens and none of us know it, not even her.

Sometimes she forgets to take her pill.

'What do the absence seizures feel like?' I asked her once.

'Like the world is a circle without a centre,' she answered.

I have always been strapped to Forget-Me-Not, in beside her twitching body.

My father was not a bad man. He was loved by lots of people. He treated many of his patients for free, or in exchange for strange gifts, like tins of pineapple juice. He did small, sweet things. We had two parrots, a lovebird and an Indian ringneck parakeet, and the parakeet loved him. Her eyes would film over when she heard his voice; she'd dash back and forth on the bottom of her cage, yelling for him. When he walked past us to take her out, crooning and stroking her feathers, she'd twist her head right back and cluck in ecstasy.

I walked into his room one day when I thought he was out and caught him lying on his bed, watching *Top Cat*. He scrambled for the remote but it was too late; I saw him decide to ride it out. He signalled to me to sit down and join him. In silence we watched the rest of the episode together. As soon as politely possible, I got up and left.

In his natty purple waistcoat and hat, Top Cat was fast-talking, improvisatory, grandiose, deluded, hopeful, ingenious, lordly in the lowest of circumstances. I really do think that's how my father saw himself. Half underdog, half god. For some time he had Che Guevara as a desktop background for his computer. 'He is our hero,' he'd say, and tell us stories about Che's magnificent revolutionary zeal.

Everyone makes compromises about who and what they count as human. George Eliot wrote:

If we had a keen vision and feeling of all ordinary human life,
it would be like hearing the grass grow and the squirrel's heart
beat, and we should die of that roar which lies on the other
side of silence.

Someone donates to Winston's Wish but looks the other way from refugees; someone fights for white women's rights but not for those of Black women; someone donates to anti-racist groups but buys prawns farmed by modern slaves. Everyone makes deals around the humanity of other people, and how consistently they allow that humanity to be present to them. That's how people make bearable homes in hostile worlds. My father was no exception. So my only issue is a personal one. In the deal that my father happened to make with his world, it was me who didn't count as human.

Fourteen years after leaving Pakistan, in theory things couldn't have been better. I'd done more than just an English A level. I'd studied literature at university, I'd got funding to do a master's and then a doctorate. And then—well beyond anything my past self could have imagined—I'd won a postdoctoral fellowship, which granted me three years of funding to finish writing my first book and start another.

But odd things kept happening to me. In the fields in my head, bones kept thrusting up from beneath, tripping me.

One day I was walking across my small living room, not wearing my glasses. Earlier in the day I'd been sitting on the red shag rug where I spent most of my time, and a little nest had gathered around me: some books, my laptop, a glass of water, blurring into the fabric. Without looking where I was going, I kicked the glass over.

The next thing I knew, I was standing very straight, gasping, my arms held tight to my sides. My face was lifted, straining away from my body, tipped up to the ceiling. My eyes had screwed tight shut. My mouth was dangling open, sucking in one breath, then another.

It was several seconds before I could unfreeze myself. I picked up the glass, which hadn't broken, and mopped up the water where it

had spilled off the rug. While I wiped the damp floor I remembered
another time, in front of colleagues, when someone had mentioned
a name that rang a bell in my head, and I'd gasped just the same
way: my body stiffening upwards, my head shooting right back. Like
I was almost underwater, gasping up to a surface which threatened
to close over me.

And I thought about the photographs of Jean-Martin Charcot's
hysteria patient Louise Augustine Gleizes—known simply as
A—who'd been raped and beaten as a child. Under hypnosis, her
body bent and arched back, as though it was remembering and
reinhabiting the poses of trauma. Being held down. Seizing in agony.

But what pose was this? What was my body remembering?

I don't know. I'll never know.

Another time, I met a colleague in the National Library of Scotland.
She was more senior than me, more experienced, and I hoped she
would become my mentor. I'd dressed nicely, calmed myself down.
It wasn't quite an interview but it wasn't just a cup of tea. The bright
sun played over the white walls and white crockery, and Morningside
ladies stopped by for tea and scones, mingling with academics and
literature enthusiasts visiting the Muriel Spark exhibition.

We talked about Spark, and D. H. Lawrence, and our shared
preoccupations, twentieth-century literature and landscape. I started
to relax. And then as I was raising my cup, suddenly—over and
across the white light of the Edinburgh day—there was my mother,
in our bedroom in Pakistan, pulling cushions down onto the floor,
packing them into the gap between beds.

The memory funnelled into me fast. I would have been perhaps
nine, Rabbit perhaps eleven. She had outgrown her child's bed.
Nothing, it seemed, could be done about this. For a while, she slept

with her feet hanging out, but eventually her legs became too long even for that. So my mother gave her own bed to Rabbit, and every night for two years, she laid cushions down on the floor and she slept there, wedged between us. In the morning she got up at 5 a.m., packed the cushions away again, and went to boil milk so it would be cool enough to drink when we awoke.

I had forgotten this.

In the National Library of Scotland, I dropped the white cup into its saucer. Tea ran everywhere, over the table and my notes and all my napkins, the little just-in-case stack I'd taken from the counter, towards the person in whose hands lay my future, or part of it.

This wasn't a good time for things to start erupting from beneath. And the thing that erupted was not useful. It wasn't useful then, and it's still not useful. It was not a meaningful piece of information. It didn't tell me anything I didn't already know. Episodes like this are the closest thing I have to flashbacks. And in themselves, they're nothing, really. My mother certainly thinks it is nothing that she slept on the floor for two years.

But that was when I realized that things were going wrong for me, in the taut, bare mesh of my world. It was another two years before I finally decided to start therapy, and my therapist gently gave me a name for the flat place I lived in.

When my father finally did me the courtesy of dying, soon after, I found myself suddenly released from the grip of his active, inexplicable disgust. And, unexpectedly, I felt adrift. There was nothing to do or not do. I'd banked on dying before I was twenty-five; before I had to live fully with the consequences of defying him. Of throwing in the towel; throwing myself on a world which—I'd been assured—would have no room for me. For a long time, spite had been keeping me afloat.

But I was past thirty, now, and still alive. And he, who had not known how to love me, was dead. Whole decades of life suddenly shoved into place in front of me, ready to be lived. A space opened up; I could hear the wind blowing.

I felt free, at last, to grapple with the question: Who and what do we love? What draws us into a relationship with a person, an object, a landscape? And what happens when that relationship goes wrong?

What stays with me: the feeling of my nails on the chicken wire. The lioness on my father's computer screen. I can't visualize faces, but I remember the red table. The grey carpet. The wooden shelving which held the decorative plate bearing a message in Arabic script which I struggled to read.

Now I live alone with the things I love. Some of them are living and some aren't. My plants. My cat. But also: my collection of stones. The things I have dug up, which last and last. The sheep skull I found at the edge of a field. One cow vertebra. One stone shaped like a cow vertebra (they sit together on the bookcase, the real and the impostor). I like bones because they speak to a basic problem of mine: that human beings are at once living, thinking, laughing creatures, and also skeletons covered in dense, marbled meat. In my efforts to understand that, people make less and less sense to me. So I collect bones, because I like knowing what everyone looks like inside.

I remember watching my friends play Go at university, and how, when no one was looking, I quietly popped a single white Go piece into my mouth. Its smooth hardness against my tongue and my palate. Where language fails, where human connection stalls, objects help. Hard china. Cold metal. Shells and bones. Things I can rub on my face, tap against my teeth, balance on my fingertip.

And it's not just beautiful or interesting things. In my fruit bowl there is an ugly chunk of wood and a seedcase covered with prickles which catches my finger every time I reach for an orange, making the hair on the back of my neck rise. I can't throw them away because I love them. To me, they're bristling with indignant, fascinating life. They live in my house, like roommates, and we don't always get on, but that's how it is.

I prefer them to human company. With human beings, your attention can't ebb and flow. You have to be fully present, all the time, until your eyes blur and your back hurts and a lump rises in your throat. With a plant, or a cat, or a stone, you can be there for a while, go away, come back.

I spent my childhood pressed up uncomfortably against other people—the people in my family—so when I got to the UK, all I wanted was to be alone. I couldn't relax when there was someone else in the room. Even when I *was* on my own, I felt someone was watching me. The smallest sound could jerk me into vigilance. People were terrifying and unpredictable, because I didn't know the things they knew, but neither did they know everything I knew, and that ignorance made them cruel. And I didn't know how to speak to them: how to hold myself, how to make conversation, how to maintain eye contact. I read books and articles about body language, and active listening, until I could pretend pretty well. But it was a lot of effort, and it exhausted me.

I loved some people, but I still couldn't bear to be near them. When they raised their hands to touch me, leaned in to kiss me, I watched them blankly. I was meant to let my body take over, but I didn't know how to do that. The surge of instinct, of rising and falling passion that other people described, never seemed to materialize. I just stood there: flat, curious, detached. Or I learned the movements expected of me—the looks, the smiles, the touches—and performed them. They had an uncanny quality which my lovers sensed. They hovered, uncertain, then fell away nervously. Or else they hung on, but I burnt out.

In *Queer Phenomenology*, the cultural theorist Sara Ahmed describes sexual orientation in terms of *orientating, as we do in space, to someone or something*, directing yourself or finding yourself directed towards them. I find this useful. I am queer because I don't orientate to any of the people the world offers me, because they are all, in the end, people. They want me to go out and laugh in a pub. They need me to be intact and coherent most of the time.

That kind of queerness is inextricable from my love for my friends. Simone Weil wrote: 'Friendship is a miracle by which a person consents to view from a certain distance, and without coming any nearer, the very being who is necessary to him as food.' Friendship builds in generous distance, hunger which accepts it will never be sated, witness without intervention. One can survive friendship when other kinds of intimacy can't be endured.

But my most intimate relationships are with things—a feeling which is different from thinking them beautiful or having sentimental attachments or associations with them. Sometimes an object is so fully and fascinatingly itself, absorbed in performing its own functions, its own presence in the world, that one can't help but love it.

Perhaps we love the things that reflect our own delusions about ourselves back to us. I love stones because they are old and hard and sure, which is how I feel, even though I am not. I love flat landscapes for much the same reason. They won't compromise. They are stiff and still, like me.

CHAPTER 2

From Ely to Welney

'We can't be nearly there,' said James, from the back seat
of the car. 'Here isn't anywhere. It's been nowhere
for miles!'
'What do you mean, James?' asked his father, driving,
with an edge to his voice.
'No up and no down,' said James, 'and no trees. Nothing.'
'It's the Fens,' his father said.

—Jill Paton Walsh, *Gaffer Samson's Luck*

I love places where there's nothing. Where, like the flat fens of
Cambridgeshire, it's nowhere for miles. Just flowered verges and
ploughed fields, from horizon to horizon. It's in these places that I
feel able to breathe—to unfurl my sticky petals, one by one—until
finally the world appears real.

I don't take that feeling for granted. Complex trauma means
that the world hardly ever feels real to me, and the more of it there
is, the less real it feels. Overwhelmed by noise, movement, the faces
of strangers, I short-circuit and recede into what psychologists
call derealization.

Derealization is a dissociative disorder often associated with
cPTSD; it makes the people and things around you seem unreal.
Judith Lewis Herman describes how 'Events continue to register in
awareness, but it is as though these events have been disconnected

from their ordinary meanings.' When I derealize, the world becomes distant and two-dimensional: a ribbon of time, where all moments exist at once, with colours, and shapes, and mouths opening and closing harmlessly. People become blurry, and I have a strong sense that they are not actually there. I see the chair they are sitting on, that existed before they arrived and will exist after they leave, and I know that at some point in the future the person *will* leave, and—since the future is as real as the present—they have, in effect, already left. This way, I can cope with whatever's happening, because I've turned the scene into an illusion. I play along, but I don't believe in it.

This has been automatic for as long as I can remember.

'It's a freeze response,' said my therapist, when I tried, haltingly, apologetically, to explain that she didn't feel real to me. We faced each other, in that small, shaded room whose teal-walled plainness had become familiar, five weeks into my therapy. 'Derealization is very, very common with complex post-traumatic stress. People have different responses to stressful situations. Fight and flight only kicks in when you might have a chance of winning, or of escaping successfully.'

Her face was as abstract and inanimate as the pot plants I kept on my bedroom windowsill. I went on listening.

'Or people might use the fawn response—being very nice and accommodating—when they think they can coax the scary thing on to their side. But if you've been in a situation where you know there's no escape, and you're physically quite small, and you can't smile yourself out of trouble—then you freeze. You go inside yourself and try to survive until things are over.'

'Like in Pakistan,' I snapped. Tears were threatening, and I avoided her gaze. I felt suddenly like the small, frightened thing she was describing, exposed in the wide leather chair.

'Yes,' my therapist said quietly. 'Because you couldn't escape your father, and your mother couldn't protect you. And you lived with a constant sense of threat. So, after a long time of this, of trauma that just goes on without ending, the freeze response becomes your default. The first resort in any stressful situation, even minor ones.'

There was a pause.

'Sometimes,' I said, curling over in my chair and staring, as usual, at the waste paper basket, 'I wonder if I'm just making all of this up.'

When I was a child, Pakistan itself felt unreal. One of the first school lessons I remember was an English language writing exercise called 'Myself.' The teacher wrote on the board: *My name is Ahmed. I am six years old. I have two sisters and one brother. My favourite subject is English.* And we all copied that down—changing the name, to *Noreen* or *Aisha* or *Salman*, but otherwise reproducing the words exactly, until we all had two sisters and one brother, and liked English best of all the subjects. Back at home, I had three sisters—I was pretty sure—but in class that didn't seem to matter. The books we read, 1960s imports from Singapore, told us that leaves turned red and gold in autumn, and snow fell in winter, even as leaves hung crisp-brown and motionless on the snowless trees outside our classroom window from August until March. Our weather didn't count. Only the weather in England counted. Far away, in picture-book fields, white children flung snowballs at each other and laughed, their pale cheeks turning pink with cold. White children were real and we were ghosts, or accidents, or something else which couldn't be acknowledged. *My name is Ahmed. I am six years old. I have two sisters and one brother. My favourite subject is English.*

But Britain, where I've lived now for seventeen years, feels unreal too. I can't quite trust in the clean water that flows from the tap; the full supermarket shelves; the orderly parks and gardens. I feel as though it's built on a lie, on hidden or delegated suffering. As though I'm in a luxurious cinema watching a film, in a city where war is raging, and over the music of the opening credits I can hear, faintly, the screams and explosions filtering through, into the cosy velvet auditorium. And there's enough truth in this, historically, to prevent me from dismissing it as mere trauma response on my part. Britain's comfortable indulgences—its infrastructure, its economy, its food supplies—depend on modern slavery, its wealth and resources on thousands of brown and Black bodies murdered during empire. Britain lives in terrible denial, I know now, of a history it can't admit to. And it survives that denial by indicating to people of colour, very subtly, very passively, that they shouldn't think of themselves as real. Because if no one real was hurt, then no real harm has been done.

Children in colonies, or ex-colonies, grow up within postcolonial trauma, thinking that their lives somehow don't exist, that they're defective shadows of the Western world. At twenty, I read an account of this for the first time, in an essay on the writer Nirad C. Chaudhuri by Amit Chaudhuri. Nirad Chaudhuri had read avidly about England, building up a grandiose mental image of the country from its most self-satisfied literature. So when he saw the white cliffs of Dover, mean and small rather than glittering and huge as they were in books, he simply could not believe that what he was seeing was real. To the colonial mind, Amit Chaudhuri argued, text had a reality which 'actual' landscape didn't. It stole my breath to realize that someone else, lots of someone elses, had had this feeling too.

Nirad Chaudhuri was a crank and an empire apologist, but his reaction to the Dover cliffs stayed with me—perhaps not in the way that he intended—as I moved through the rest of my education, and through a world which went on refusing to cohere with my understanding of what was true. As I finished my doctoral degree in Oxford—checking footnotes, rearranging sections of my thesis, running from one college to another to teach, applying to job after job—I acquired a twitch in my right eye, a deepening of the pain in my joints and stomach that I'd struggled with in Cambridge, and an increasingly fragile sense of reality. Oxford is a surreal place at the best of times, and I was drawing close to the end of something which, to my younger self, had seemed beyond the bounds of possibility: a humanities education which was rich and thick and nourishing, sustained by government grants and college scholarships. I'd been operating in the realm of the unreal, the too-good-to-hope-for, for some time by this point. I'd outrun the uncanny veil of my childhood, but now it seemed to be catching up with me, and I felt myself starting to crack.

My doctoral thesis was on the poetry of Stevie Smith. I'd noticed that Smith's writing kept returning to the flat fens of Eastern England. Once largely underwater, filled with wild and mysterious life—otters, godwits, ragwort, crayfish, voles, bitterns, eels, newts, bats, cuckoos—they've long since been seeded, respectably, with peas, sugar beet and canola. And yet a vast sky still arches over them, dotted with clouds or masked in rain, streaked with orange sunset or purple sunrise. In the fenlands, the celestial, the mythical, seemed to lie cheek to cheek with the earthen everyday world. The fens, I thought, might help me understand how to feel about my life, my memory, as it negotiated clumsily between the real and the unreal, one turning into the other and back again. With my viva looming, I began planning a trip. I would walk along the Hereward Way: a hundred-mile path, stretching from Norfolk to Rutland. Or rather—because I was so easily tired, from the pain which still roams through my knees and elbows and stomach—I would walk a very small piece of it, from Ely to Welney. About eleven miles.

It's research, I told my friends. No, you can't come. Not this time.

That summer, after I'd passed my viva, I packed up my room in Oxford and boarded a train to Ely, watching the landscape flatten and spread as it moved eastwards. The low hedgerows blurred into a pale green strip as the train sped past. Every now and then a bouquet of multicoloured graffiti flashed up, fat letters sprayed out in red, green and orange. For several minutes—because, as I was learning, things take time in the fens to vanish from sight—I watched a squat pair of industrial cement chimneys huffing pleasantly into the big sky. And over, far in the distance, a little flock of wind turbines was waving at me. The thick, plum-grey cloud overhead began to give way to bright, well-washed sunlight.

I knew myself. There was no point pretending that this was more than the most moderate of adventures. I'd never understood direction, never been able to give directions, even, mortifyingly, to my own home. That part of my brain was warped and foetal, and would never get any bigger, because I hadn't been able to stretch it as a child. Nice girls don't walk in the street where men can see them.

So I had to be realistic about what my journey would look like. I couldn't strike out into the fens, armed only with some mint cake and a map. That would be melodramatic for anyone. It would be positively dangerous for a small, flat girl with no sense of direction, who got dizzy and worn out in the afternoons and had strange pains in the furthest parts of her body. I'd step into the flatlands in the smallest way, starting with an Airbnb in Ely, and the 'Popular Walks' section of the 'Visit Ely' website. And if I needed to, I would stop and drink a cup of tea from my Thermos and play on my phone like a numb teenager, while the proper nature people marched past me with maps in plastic pockets round their necks.

Each 'Popular Walk' had a pamphlet, downloadable as a PDF, describing it in an elaborately curled font which someone had presumably, at some point, considered a good idea. I spread the one for the Hereward Way out on the train table. My plan was to begin at the west door of Ely Cathedral and end my journey at the Lamb and Flag pub in Welney. The ritual precision of starting at the west door appealed to me. It felt like the setting of a spell. Sun streamed and puddled on the table—I'd got a section of four seats, all to myself—and I smiled out at the green-brown landscape that split my window in one stark lovely line.

In the back of the carriage someone was talking on their phone. They weren't speaking loudly, or being obnoxious, but after a while something they said caught my ear, mixed in with the sunlight and the landscape and the red train seats, and I found myself listening.

'It's cheaper for him to go to Spain just to get those cigarettes. I think he probably has his kids go through customs with their coat pockets stuffed full of them!'

The man laughed. I pressed the heels of my hands into my eyes and my forehead into the table.

I was about seven. Playing quietly in the corner of the room with some small plastic animals, my back to the adults. My mother was packing knitwear, smelling cosily of mothballs, into a suitcase.

'You put it in the children's shoes.' My father was standing, looking down at my mother as she worked. 'You make pads of it—wrapped in plastic—and lift up the inside sole and put it underneath. cling film, not a plastic bag, understood? Or it will make a noise. And no one will look. Yes?'

My mother made the sound which meant yes, which meant submission, even if not agreement. I'd stopped playing, though I knew not to turn round. Sickness was spreading through my stomach, a burn running up into my elbows.

The next morning, as I got dressed for the plane journey, my shoes looked normal. I put them on and wiggled my toes without really meaning to—I was frightened both to know and not to know—but I couldn't feel anything. Later, I walked through the airport with my mother and sisters, feeling one foot floating up after the other, knowing not to look down. And at the end of the journey, after we'd landed and been hugged and plied with biscuits, I left my shoes by the door and made sure not to return to them until the following morning.

I cannot answer any more questions about this.

'Yeah! Exactly, yeah!' The man was laughing harder now, almost choking with it. 'And then you make your money back on the buffet and the fishbowls!'

As the train sped along, I couldn't stop thinking about those tiny shoes. White Bubblegummers trainers with red detail and laces. Perhaps the whole episode was something I'd dreamt; I had no way of proving otherwise. I stayed frozen with the memory lodged in my cheekbones, just below my open, tearless eyes, as the long flat line of Cambridgeshire reeled itself out beside me.

I didn't start to unfreeze till the train pulled into Ely. I bumbled around the station, turning my map of Ely one way, then the other, and somehow got myself and my backpack to my Airbnb, encased all the time in a coat too hot and tight for the sunny day. The key was hidden inside a ceramic Minnie Mouse by the front doorstep, and even though I was sharing the house with other guests I managed to reach my room without bumping into anyone.

After I'd unpacked, I ventured into the kitchen to make tea. From the window, I could see a sunny car park, and beyond, the spire of Ely Cathedral rising up. The 'ship of the fens,' as it's known, stretching upwards and breaking the flat horizon. People latch on to it gratefully as they gaze across the landscape: a focal point, a moment of relief from the endless fenland. At the same time, the cathedral seemed to guarantee or reinforce the levelness of the landscape. Without the contrast of the spire piercing upwards, would the fens seem less flat?

I was thinking too quickly, moving too quickly, so that I could get back to my room; I prised a teabag out of one of the identical grey caddies lined up along the kitchen counter, soaked it and pressed it hastily on the side of the mug. When I threw it into the bin, it left amber drips on the lino which I wiped up roughly with my bare hand. The thought of running into another guest just then—of having to smile and focus on their face—sent my skin shuddering. Everything felt very distant, like I was standing on an island, staring out across the water.

Ely used to be an actual island, and the area's still called the Isle of Ely. In the past, when the fens flooded and the waters rose, a fen dweller might suddenly have found themselves marooned, alone. Fine. A memory had come rushing in, and had left me there, cut off from everything.

What would I have said, if someone had asked me what was wrong? *I think I might have been used as a mule to smuggle something, once, but I don't know for sure.*

I can never know for sure.

There's an Old English poem, 'Wulf and Eadwacer,' set in the fenlands, which captures this feeling of paralysed, helpless uncertainty. It's very difficult to translate and skips between genres. It might be a riddle, or an elegy, or a ballad. I first read it when I was eighteen, and it was as mysterious to me as to the scholars who've puzzled over it for decades. But when I read it, even in translation, I feel myself reflected. In the poem, the unnamed speaker finds herself separated from her beloved Wulf by the soaking wild landscape and by a terrifying, mysterious army.

It is to my people as if someone gave them a gift.
They want to kill him, if he comes with a troop.
It is different for us.

Wulf is on one island I on another.
That island, surrounded by fens, is secure.
There on the island are bloodthirsty men.
They want to kill him, if he comes with a troop.
It is different for us.

I thought of my Wulf with far-wandering hopes,
Whenever it was rainy weather, and I sat tearfully,
Whenever the warrior bold in battle encompassed me with his arms.
To me it was pleasure in that, it was also painful . . .

The refrain beats in my head, even more haunting in the Old English: *Ungelic is us.* Unlike is us. We are different; we are separated; it is different for us.

It's hard to see clearly in this murky fenland poem. Is Wulf the woman's lover? He might, some scholars think, be her child. And who is the mysterious Eadwacer, creeping up on these two?

Do you hear, Eadwacer? A wolf is carrying
our wretched whelp to the forest,
that one easily sunders which was never united:
our song together.

Everything should be clearly visible in a flat landscape like this. But identities seem to shift and get scrambled. Might Wulf and Eadwacer be the same person? What is real, and what isn't? Who is the loved? Who the feared? Might they be rolled into one?

Us on that island in Pakistan, my mother and sisters and me, wrapped up in the chicken wire which ran over our windows. *It is different for us.* Staring out at the murky landscape beyond, where things moved and whispered and shifted, and one could never know for sure what was happening, or how one was implicated. Me on another island now, a wretched whelp by myself, wrapped in my own cramping body. Not knowing how to explain to myself why I still felt the chicken wire closing around me.

The fens bound the possible and the impossible, the everyday and the fantastic, into one inscrutable plane. Reading 'Wulf and Eadwacer' felt like staring into a mirror. Imagination and reality blurred together. There was no way of retracing history's steps to find the 'real' self I could have had.

I took my tea up to my room and fell asleep.

The next morning, things went wrong almost at once. I hadn't slept well, and so I was sick with pain: that old daily burning, through my elbows and my tailbone and my knees, which no doctor could explain. Freud might have called it hysteria, and that morning I did feel hysterical. I stuffed everything back into my bag, buckled it round my chest and hip bones, and shoved myself out of the house.

I'd passed a little antique shop the day before, and for some reason I turned into it now, on my way to the cathedral. To give myself a moment's grace, I realized, as I worked out which way I needed to walk. I'd expected to see the cathedral rising up above the rooftops, to orientate me, but from this angle it was invisible. The most important thing, I thought, was not to panic: to take a moment and perhaps see if there was anything nice in here for my friends. I bent over the rings on the counter, then turned and scanned a clear plastic curtain of pouches, holding medals, and brooches, and—I knew before I'd reached them, somehow, I don't know how. I knew they'd be there. A whole collection of golliwog badges, one in each compartment. Seven pounds each.

I made a strange sound, strange even to myself, and swung towards the counter, where the shopkeeper was still studiously looking through papers. After a moment, though, I turned round and walked out of the shop. A man was folding cardboard boxes just outside, packing them into a bin. He smiled at me, warmly. I didn't smile back. My whole face was stiff, as though I'd been crying, and my jaw was taut and my stomach felt about to harden and fall off. It didn't matter what anyone said, or did. How much they smiled.

Somehow I found the spire of Ely Cathedral, and got myself up there, not very much past quarter to ten. But then I couldn't find the west window, where I was meant to start my walk, because I didn't really understand what west was. Falling at the first hurdle, shattering the spell of the precise instructions. I asked a passer by for guidance, though I couldn't understand his answer, and then a group of ladies, failing to hide the quaver in my voice. Upset, already.

'Are you all right, dear?' The ladies were eyeing me with concern. 'You mustn't worry too much. All the windows in the cathedral are beautiful, whether west or east or anything else.'

By the time I had arranged myself on the right side of the cathedral, I wanted my legs to give way under me, to sleep my way out of the situation. This wasn't how this was meant to go. I'd come to the fens to feel at home, to spend time in an environment which would reflect myself back to me. But already this world was pulling me under, turning me somersaulting in a vague and distant sea.

I focused on getting out of Ely, ignoring the guidebook and throwing myself more or less in the direction I was meant to go. My head felt like a huge room; I'd retreated to the back of it, operating my face and hands with long awkward levers. It wasn't till I'd reached the suburbs that I was able to untwist out of myself enough to see what was going on. A flash of red caught my eye, and I stopped. It was an old-fashioned postbox, standing in someone's garden, its door invitingly open, a basket of red geraniums hanging inside. Next to it stood a real, small tractor, with a large ceramic collie sitting up at the wheel, and a Union Jack dangling limp on a flagpole. Two stone lions guarded the front door. There was something very odd about the whole arrangement. It nagged at me.

I walked on. Suburbs are always weird; we've been taught to find them so. Brown houses with little red flashes in the brickwork, and grey slate roofs, and on the pavements almost no one at all: just quiet parked cars leaning up against the kerb. And in each house, fond little touches of individuality. One had a low white fence with a curly ironwork pattern. Another had a bush cut into a huge bird, with a sharp beak and tail, meticulously smooth. The owners must have had to pop out every morning with a cup of tea and a pair of shears to give it a touch-up.

Then—a few houses later—I spotted another garden postbox. And then another. They were everywhere. And why not, after all? Who wouldn't want a shiny red postbox in their garden? But combined with the golliwog badges, and the flag, and the stone lions, all this British iconography, heaping up and up, suddenly seemed so nervous: like an Irish pub in Germany or America or Singapore, festooned with more shamrocks and leprechauns than you'd ever see in Ireland proper. Here I was in Britain, and yet the country seemed unsure of itself. Its identity had to be enforced: stamped and restamped onto a place which kept shifting and turning. A flat place is somewhere that can't be relied upon to stay, consistently, where you left it. People tried to brand it with anxious bits of national tat. But in the end they just disintegrated or fluttered away, leaving the place alone, itself, unchanged.

By the time I'd managed to put these thoughts into words in my mind, I was well out of the city, and I'd been walking through the level fields for some time. The crisp horizon, the empty stretch of green and brown. The crops in the field next to me sat very low. I felt suddenly that I had become tiny, and that I was walking across a brown front-door mat. I stopped and unfurled the map, where I'd traced the Hereward Way in pink.

The path is named after Hereward the Wake, an eleventh-century English nobleman who's supposed to have roamed the fens—Cambridgeshire, Lincolnshire, Norfolk—leading local opposition to the Norman invasion, with a base in the city of Ely. I like this story for several reasons. When one is marched—I suppose—through the kings and queens of England at school, or when (as a worried little born-abroader) one flicks back and forth through the tiny *Collins Guide to the Kings and Queens of England*, trying to get a grasp on the country, what falls quietly by the wayside are the shadow histories, the figures defeated. William the Conqueror pops up, suddenly, in 1066, and history skews off one way, leaving an alternative history to die. Hereward and the Fenlanders fight in vain, sinking slowly into the wet marshes, out of sight.

There are few details about Hereward's life. This is convenient, in a way: legend and speculation have rushed in to fill the gaps. He's meant to have been born in Lincolnshire. But he was exiled for disruptive behaviour—including (perhaps) drunkenness, housebreaking, and stealing a horse from a monk—and made an outlaw at eighteen. Hereward ended up in Flanders after legendary exploits in Cornwall, Ireland and Northumbria. At one point he's supposed to have fought a half-human bear, though this doesn't matter to the story.

'An outlaw! Like you!' my best friend had teased, when I told her this before leaving for my trip. 'Except the most disruptive thing you do is glare. You're a very moderate outlaw.'

'And I was sixteen, not eighteen.' I was enjoying being teased. 'And being an outlaw sounds much more poetic than being disowned.'

When Hereward returned to England, he found that his father's lands had been seized by Normans, and his younger brother killed. In 1070, four years after William's invasion, Hereward took part in an anti-Norman insurrection at Ely. Though his collaborator was arrested, Hereward and his followers escaped and continued their resistance from the wild fenlands.

The myths get more and more outrageous. Hereward infiltrated the Norman camp, disguised as a potter, then as a fisherman. He set fire to a wooden tower from which a witch was trying to cast spells on him. When he retreated, a huge white wolf guided him through the marshland. It's all very dramatic: a heroic underdog story. In the nineteenth century, Charles Kingsley (best known for writing *The Water-Babies*) turned Hereward into a highly romantic figure in his 1898 novel *Hereward the Wake*:

> . . . the [Fenlanders] disdained to yield to the Norman invader.
> For seven long years they held their own, not knowing, like
> true Englishmen, when they were beaten; and fought on
> desperate . . . Their bones lay white on every island in the fens;
> their corpses rotted on gallows beneath every Norman keep . . .
> But they never really bent their necks to the Norman yoke . . .
> Most gallant of them all . . . was Hereward the Wake . . .

Kingsley's fantasy of English underdog-ness, and his language of colonization, is ironic, particularly because he's writing at the end of the nineteenth century, when England itself was intently colonizing everything it could find. Like everyone else at every point in history, Kingsley seems unable to see what appears, in hindsight, to offer itself fully to sight. Not that accuracy was anywhere on Kingsley's priority list. Does this fantasy of a gallant defender—his face 'of extraordinary beauty,' of 'immense breadth of chest and strength of limb'—intersect at any point with historical fact? Unlikely. Hereward was little more than a useful way of building a British self-image of courage, tenacity and heroism. And though Hereward has been memorialized, he'll never be central to the popular imagination around the Norman invasion: there's no Hereward featured on the Bayeux Tapestry. Walking the Hereward Way, I was following a path paying tribute to a history that didn't happen. Stepping into the slipstream of a semi-fictitious figure, half submerged in myth. No wonder I needed that clear pink line to navigate these blurry territories.

Jon McGregor closes his book of short stories set in the fens, *This Isn't The Sort Of Thing That Happens To Someone Like You*, with a litany of placenames that he calls 'Memorial Stone,' sorted by their suffixes:

Scrafield, Stainfield, Bitchfield, Kelfield, Gorefield.

Wildsworth, Hawksworth, Pickworth, Colsterworth, Stainton by Langworth, Potterhanworth, Cold Hanworth, Faldingworth, Tamworth Green, West Barkwith, East Barkwith, Benniworth, Butterwick, Susworth, West Stockwith, Ailsworth, East Stockwith, Epworth, Langworth, Epworth Turbary.

Ticks Moor, West Moor.

Gayton le Marsh, Chapel Six Marshes, Marshchapel,
Holbeach Marsh.

The repetition is soothing, like a spell or a chant. Yet it's also
grounding: the more a place can be labelled, the more controlled
and predictable it seems. These featureless places drive the desire to
name, to catalogue, to manage. One needs a map to feel in charge.

I have never been any good at reading maps.

I scanned the words on mine—Fox's Drove, Redcaps Lane,
Three R's Farm, storybook names for a spellbound, spellbinding
landscape—and went on walking.

The fields began to brighten as I moved over the land, step by
step becoming clearer. In the places where sun came through the
clouds, the crops flushed into light, patchily. Their shine moved with
the clouds, shifting to mirror the light in the sky above. Nothing
is as magnificent as starkness. A bold line. A strong bright colour.
Or this fearless severing of earth and sky, in the flat fens, with a
single sweeping horizon. Things may be prettier or more beautiful,
but nothing catches me in the chest like a landscape which cuts
itself, unapologetically, into one's vision: not troubling to entertain
or to amuse its viewer. A flat landscape simply *is*, with an intensity
which excludes you as you stand and gaze. You are in the presence
of something which seems to radiate courage and independence.
Something eccentric, also, which refuses to perform beauty in
predictable ways. Unvarying, and perhaps a little absurd in its
stubborn insistence. And all the more lovable for that.

I passed by a field of what I thought might be rapeflowers, with
small yellow heads. They clustered close and thick, as though they
were whispering, eyeing me up. I gave them their privacy, leaving
them to conspire. Once, these fields had been a peaty, waterlogged
marshland. Huge beds of sedge and reeds alternated with willow

trees. Eels writhed between the tall grasses that stuck up out of the rippling water; herons picked their way daintily through the meres. Well into the seventeenth century, human beings lived around the edges of the fens, on the fen islands and the silt banks; they fished, gathered reeds, hunted waterfowl, carved out chunks of rich peat. The area had a reputation for being wild and riddled with malaria, or 'marsh fever,' which drove many wealthier people away. It made the land, thick with peat and water and grass, a good place to hide. No wonder Hereward and his followers liked it.

But the fens are now overwhelmingly tamed. After centuries of trial and error, the water has been drained away, leaving only flatland. Most of it is farmed. Only a tiny fraction remains as wild fen, broken up and dispersed amidst the cultivation.

The farmed land is covered with a complex system of ditches and drains, more than 25,000 kilometres of them. They fit over this ground like a tight net, keeping it in place, keeping it intact. Even so, disaster can strike at any moment. In the past, the people who lived here stayed vigilant. Ready, at any time, for floods. When one came, it came fast. The great flood of 1947 kept parts of the fens underwater for two months, and many homes were evacuated. Families were cut off and relied on Sea Cadets in dinghies and canoes to ferry food to them.

Today, flash floods hit the area regularly. Photos circulate on social media most years: Vans driving wheel-deep through flooded streets, sending white spray off on both sides. Water rising to lap at the edges of gardens, spilling through the entrance to Tesco. From a distance, roads shine and shimmer.

This was familiar to me. Lahore flooded every year, when the monsoon came. Without a system of drainage, the brick-dry land was quickly overwhelmed. It couldn't hold the water, which rose feet at a time. The street on the way to school became a river. Staff arranged bricks to jut above the water level, and we hopped from one to the next, one arm extended for balance, the other clutching our backpacks. But the water receded almost as soon as it arrived, under the hot steady sun, leaving only a memory. In Britain, water lingers. It creeps cold into walls, into bones, eating slowly away at anything it touches.

As sea levels rise, scientists predict that large parts of Cambridgeshire will be submerged more and more often. Ely will become an island once more, though it will lose parts of its suburbs to the flood. Meanwhile the town of March, beyond Welney, will vanish completely. I thought about this too as I walked, imagined flat water effacing the flat land which stretched crisp-cut between the ends of my vision. On the horizon, low dark trees formed a beaded edge.

On my left, the hedge broke. The pale green field beyond had been ploughed first one way then another: a single tree on the horizon sat with a shadow parked under it. In the corner of the field, just by the path, was a brown pool. *Buffalo wallow*, my brain supplied, before I could think, and a shiver went over me. In the sun, in this moment of stillness, the dry, yellow grass, the rubble of ploughed earth, called up my grandfather's farm in Pakistan, where buffalo heads poked up from deep pools. When he wasn't lying on his bed or shuffling up and down the corridors of our house in Lahore, he went to his farm outside the city and lay on a *charpai* there instead. On Fridays, we occasionally piled into the car and drove out to see him.

I stood on the path, at the edge of the buffalo-wallow-that-wasn't. Now that I'd realized what I was thinking, things started to fit together. On the other side of the path, there was a little ditch, and what it reminded me of—what it had been reminding me of, I realized now, for some time—was a little ditch on the farm, running with a bit of brown water, that I used to call the river.

Grass grew on its sides, and tiny flowers. I was allowed to walk along the ditch for perhaps half a kilometre on my own, picking the tiny flowers, feeling like a child in a book. A white child, of course, like Milly-Molly-Mandy or someone in Enid Blyton. A real child. It was the kind of thing they did, those real children in books. 'I'm going for a walk by the river,' I'd announce. My mother would nod.

The ditch was where I walked, at the farm, when something was happening that I didn't want to know about. A fight. A visitor. Most of all, when my father was issuing some haphazard and terrifying instruction to my older sisters. Like when they were ten, and he decided it was time to teach them to use a gun. I walked along the 'river,' staring down at the ground and listening to gunshots in the distance.

In the fens, the sun started tucking itself back under the edges of grey cloud, and the patches of cropped ground turned from brown to a heathery purple. Banded with green, the land looked almost plush under the softening grey sky. A scratch of white caught my eye: white feathers, disarranged, and in the middle of the bundle a small ribcage sticking up, the size of a child's fist. I struggled briefly with my desire to pick up the bones and take them with me. In the end, I turned away, reminding myself that all those feathers meant there might still be organs attached. Things might crawl up from them and over me. So I left the bird to be pecked clean.

Over to my right, now, I could hear machinery making its unhurried way over the field; to the left, a distant plane. Blackberries weighed down the hedges. Some were melting, already, into wine. Others were still bound tight, like heads in hairnets. Overhead, the quiet clack of pylons, doing whatever it is that pylons do nowadays.

There had been pylons for some time, swooping up and up through the fields, silver wires trailing between them. Like bridesmaids holding a train. Or a line of old ladies squatting ankle-deep with their skirts pulled up. In Lahore there were pylons everywhere, criss-crossing overhead, but I was startled when I arrived in Britain and found that there were none to see in my town.

'Mostly they put the wires underground here,' said my mother, which seemed insane to me. What happened when you wanted to repair them?

In the fens the pylons held up the empty sky, stopping it from collapsing on the land. They kept the flat from the flat, making a wide and soaring space through which I could walk. Eventually, the purple gave way to bare, bright green. A green so vivid I could feel it almost physically against my cheek, cold and fragrant and damp. Enough green to fill both my eyes many times over. And it stayed there with me, as I walked, for miles.

What I noticed—pausing for a moment outside a farm—was that I didn't feel any pressure about how or where to look. The summer before, I'd made my way around Hadrian's Wall with a friend, winding over the undulating land. The wall twisted up over a peak, and I made it to the top, knees screaming and stomach cramping, just as the sun was setting over the Northumberland countryside. Gasping for breath, I turned to see the pink fields and dips and swells of landscape. And I felt a lance of pain, a different kind. I knew that scene was the most beautiful thing I had seen that year. I knew it would be a memory that my future self, old and immobile, would be glad of; would hoard against the cold nights. But I felt completely unequal to it. I couldn't look at it long enough or in the right way, I couldn't drink it in the way that I thought I ought to. I couldn't stop myself tiring and turning away from a scene which, in a few decades time, I would give my eyeteeth to glimpse for a second.

That beauty asked too much of me. I couldn't love it as much as it deserved. My friend caught up with me, panting.

'Wow,' he said, turning slowly to take in the view. 'That's something else, isn't it.' And I couldn't really tell what he was thinking.

In the fens, there was no pain of any kind. It had lapsed at some point since Ely. The fens weren't beautiful in the way that Northumberland was beautiful. But I knew that, here, there was no right or wrong way to look. I could just be with the landscape, be in it. And because the landscape was the same for miles and miles, I could give it the time it needed. I didn't have to 'take it all in' at once. I could let it seep slowly into me as I walked. I could get to know it, like a dear friend, over a long time, rather than forcing a sudden overwhelming intimacy which couldn't be sustained.

Most of the signs I had come across on the road read simply PASSING PLACE. They imagined, over and over, a situation where there wasn't enough space for two things, two cars to coexist. And yet there was plenty of space in this landscape, for me to pass, to move or run or lie down in any way I wanted. The whole horizon was my passing place.

Things changed when I turned along the New Bedford River. First of all, this was an artificial river, so I was immediately and unjustly suspicious. The river dates back to the drainage of the fens, perhaps the most banal drama of British history. Before the drainage, the fens were flooded either permanently or seasonally, with only islands like Ely poking up through the water. Though eels, waterfowl, reeds and sedge provided an ample living for the Fenlanders, the British crown was preoccupied with the fertile agricultural land beneath the floodwaters. They longed to bring that land to the surface, to profit from it economically, and to demonstrate their power to subjugate nature, to manipulate earth and water alike. Nature would be forced to play by culture's rules. In the seventeenth century, Cornelius Vermuyden—an expert who'd played a large part in the draining of the Netherlands—was brought in by the court of Charles I with the express purpose of draining the marshes. He divided the fenlands into three sections, or 'levels'—an ironic name, given the identical level at which most of that land sits today—and cut in the Bedford Rivers to drain out the water.

I sat down on the top of the bank. A few minutes ago, swans had been making their way down Engine Basin. Now, big upright lumps of white foam sailed along this river, away from the pumping station that ground away behind me. Honking white geese flew low overhead and settled on a field, among other white creatures that I'd thought were sheep. Distance made everything strange. After a while, even the pumping station fell quiet.

In the seventeenth century the Fenlanders hated the new canals. Horrified at the loss of their livelihoods, they tried to sabotage the drainage efforts at every turn. They ripped down dykes, set fire to reedbeds and attacked wind pumps. But the drainage went on year after painful year, decade after decade, battling the shrinking peat and changes in the weather. Cornelius Vermuyden would not live to see it complete. But finally, with the advent of steam-powered pumps in the nineteenth century, the fens were emptied of water, and with it much of their biodiversity, leaving behind only the flat lands. Without brutal human intervention, these landscapes I was walking through—heart thudding, breath catching—would never have existed. Perhaps it was odd of me, even perverse, to love a beauty predicated on destruction, thousands of animal and plant species wiped out by the wealthy and powerful.

I began to understand that the intensity I loved in this landscape—its poised, puzzling insistence on its ungiving self—depended on that water, held up by that bank. The drains and the dykes had created the landscape. And they kept it as it was, stretched flat and taut as a drumskin.

It is not advisable, noted the guide, *to fall into the drains.*

Eventually the trees opened out on my right, giving way to flat land and sky, and the stretched triangle of the road—base at my feet, apex at the horizon—was reflected in a long, streaming triangle of cloud, ribboning overhead. The governing shape of the fens: an arrowhead pointing to the horizon. A horizon that is never reached.

Polderblindness. That's what they call it in the Netherlands, when you've been driving through the flatlands, or polders, so long that your perceptions of time and space collapse; you can no longer react quickly enough, in the case of a sudden obstacle. A couple of hours in, my feet were no longer touching the ground. The sun was high in the sky, and I felt as though a plumb line ran down from it to the crown of my head, holding me up. I was moving my legs, feebly, suspended in mid air, like one of those old Hollywood films where the car stays still while the scenery moves around it. I was real, but nothing else was.

As I'd walked, I'd become weightless. I merged into my environment and loomed out again. There was nothing in my head but that clear line of the horizon, encircling me. I knew I needed to arrive in Welney in time to check in at the Lamb and Flag by 10 p.m. The receptionist and I would need to coincide in time. But until then, until I reached Welney, there was nothing to coincide with. Just me and the vast landscape. Time came from other things. The watch on my wrist. I unbuckled it and put it in my backpack, then turned my phone off and dropped that in too. Once I'd done this, the only marker of time was the sky, glowing white and darkening to grey, letting loose little handfuls of rain. I imagined it was a big bowl, a brimming bowl of white water, suspended upside down, and that I was a little water boatman skiing across its surface.

I don't know how long I walked that day. It felt as though I didn't really walk at all. It was as if my episodes of derealization found physical form in that landscape. The topography expressed my experience of a world which, continually, turned human faces into disconnected bundles of colours, my friends' voices into sounds which drifted without touching me.

At some point, though, I realized that I'd been absently eyeing a speck on the horizon for some time, watching as it swelled and doubled. Gradually it formed into two walkers, with their Nordic sticks and a nice brown dog with a puffy forehead, until we were close enough to speak. They greeted me warmly. My mouth turned up at one side, uneasily.

'Hello! Nice day for it!' They were stopping. Why were they stopping? Without another option, I slowed down too. They dropped their packs and smiled at me, unwrapping cereal bars. 'Where are you off to?'

'Welney,' I said unwillingly.

'Ah! For the wetland centre?'

'No. Just . . . to look.'

'What, then—just—a tour of the fens?'

'Sort of, yes.' I decided to try and be brave. 'I'm interested in flat landscapes.'

The walkers looked puzzled, then rallied themselves. 'Well, quite right! There's lots to look at here if you look close enough! Water beetles, voles; species you don't get anywhere else. Do you like birds? The birdwatching round here is amazing.'

I did like birds. But I felt we were getting off the point. I didn't want lots to look at, not even voles or water beetles.

The man launched into a speech—something about weevils—and no matter how much I twisted and stared at the ground, he kept talking, as the woman laughed and shook her head indulgently at me, trying to catch my eye.

Even after they'd shouldered their packs and waved goodbye, I felt queasy. From then on, for miles, every time I turned back, I knew those two would be there. Turning speck-like again, in the end, but still visible. Still, thoughtlessly, trapping me with their ideas about what mattered and didn't matter; taking my fenlands and ripping up their beautiful flatness in a noisy search for weevils. But as I walked on, I found, to my own surprise, that it was okay. I was able to put them out of my mind. The flat landscape outweighed them. They became another unimportant detail, as irrelevant as the tiny trees or the stars of scattered meadow flowers by the road. Or the weevils, busy with their own lives.

The concept of *nature* as distinct from *culture* emerged in the seventeenth and eighteenth centuries, thanks to the Scientific Revolution. Scientists such as Francis Bacon positioned nature as something to be looked at, studied, analysed and controlled by humans, who were above and apart from it. Man, Bacon thought, is 'Nature's agent and interpreter.' Nature, meanwhile, 'is conquered only by obedience.' Culture could study nature in order to control and manipulate it to its ends. This nature–culture divide came to echo other oppositions, like *nature* and *nurture*; *genuine* and *artificial*; *real* and *unreal*. In other words: there's an original, pure way of things, and then there's the result of human intervention.

All these binaries—and the values that society attaches to them—haunt each other. In Cambridgeshire, Ely is culture: buildings, people. It towers over the fens. Plants, earth, water: these, in contrast, are nature.

Bacon argued culture was a triumph over nature, like Ely Cathedral, the triumphant ship sailing through its conquered territories. Others, like Rousseau, cast nature as the superior counterpart to floundering, man-made culture. 'Natural' children, Rousseau thought, were wise until ruined by the interference of 'cultured' adults. 'Everything is good as it comes from the hands of the Author of Nature,' he writes in *Émile*, 'but everything degenerates in the hands of man.'

Whether we tend to agree with Rousseau or Bacon, we know, really, that there's no simple opposition between nature and culture. Humans are part of nature, and organic life worms its way into the most built-over environments. We think of places like the fens as rural, and yet that flatness derives from intensive human intervention. The fens were drained at great effort and expense; the smooth green landscape they left behind is kept that way with high walls, regular inspections, dredging of canals. Nature and culture intertwine indissolubly in the fenlands, as in every person. What happened to you silts invisibly into any original, natural self that predated it. In the end, you are who you are.

The light was shifting, in the way it does as early afternoon turns to late; the sun seemed to slap its knees with both hands, preparing to stand up and leave. I turned off the road and walked into the middle of a field to have my lunch. It was mushy underfoot; if I stood still for more than a couple of moments, water rose up around my shoe, with a coldness that threatened my dry socks. I wandered around, aimlessly, unable to find anywhere to sit, and eventually I perched on a wooden fence to eat my sandwich. The weather had hardened with the loss of the sun, shifting abruptly to cold, wet wind. I couldn't pour tea, not balanced on that little wooden rail, so I took out my Thermos and hugged it. It was a bad Thermos, from Poundland, and heat leaked from it like a hot-water bottle. I'd been warned about this by the 'Popular Walk' guide, that icy winds could pour fast across this vast landscape, unhindered by hill or forest, nothing to slow them down. I crouched, fishing thick wool jumpers out of my backpack, and trudged on towards Welney, a ball of fuzz.

As I walked, I realized my hands were cradling my woolly belly, the way they often do unprompted when I'm alone. Since I was tiny, everything bad that has happened to me has taken up residence in my stomach in the form of knots, and clots, and long sore nerves, and nausea, and other feelings I don't understand. I'm uncertain where my stomach begins and where it ends. It is a huge incomprehensible blur in the middle of my body.

My father could not understand why my stomach always hurt. I remember lying on my back on the floor, staring up at him as he poked me with two hard fingers. He paused and gave me a twist of a smile. 'I can feel your backbone,' he said. And went on poking.

Every time I looked at the broad reaches of space and the clouds—grey underneath, white on top, solid and almost cubic—I found my chest filling with breath. And with that breath—I imagined—my body expanded, spreading out freely and limply over the fields, as far as it needed. Two ploughed lines wove through the field, mirroring the bank and the horizon. My stomach moved outwards as I breathed in, away from my spine, as though it felt safe to explore a little. My body took up all the space that it wanted, and with every exhale I returned to myself, small and long-legged, walking quietly over the flat land. I felt powerfully myself. That self

was awkward, like a badly assembled marionette, singed around
the edges, solitary and hostile. And there was room for me, in that
moment, to be all of those things, without apology.

Then a sign. LAMB AND FLAG, NEXT LEFT. Somehow I'd done
it. I was nearly in Welney. Fifteen minutes and a very frightening
A-road later, I was pushing the door open to a blast of warm air and
bewildering chatter.

'How was your walk?'

The woman behind the bar pulled another tray of steaming,
dripping glasses out of the dishwasher. An older man in the corner
was listening too. I nursed my Coke, very conscious of my scraggly
legs, my big nose, the fact that I was the only brown person in the pub,
and tried to frame a response. The walk was something I'd needed
to do, and which had been very special to me. But it sat outside any
judgement I could convey logically. I couldn't say if I was refreshed
or energized. I wasn't sure that the walk could be said to have done
any of the things a walk is meant to do: offer scenery, adventure, an
escape from the daily round, from the inside of one's head.

'It was so cold!' I shuddered theatrically, and the woman behind
the bar laughed, turning to chat to the next customer. Safely ignored,
I buried my nose in my glass and went on thinking. In some ways
I felt very sad and very raw, and deeply inside my own head. As
though I'd spent time reaffirming a bare, stony truth which was my
reality, and which couldn't coexist with happiness. But why do we
assume that happiness is the best thing one can aspire to? Perhaps
I'd rather feel real by myself than feel happy and integrated into a
world that felt unreal to me. Sara Ahmed writes about the pressure
on women, in particular, to be happy, and how happiness can come
at great cost:

the happiness duty for women is about the narrowing of horizons, about giving up an interest in what lies beyond the familiar . . . imagination is what allows women to be liberated from happiness . . . We might want . . . girls to read the books that enable them to be overwhelmed with grief.

I'd rather be grief-stricken than feel unreal. The landscape had made me feel human, somewhere on the spectrum of human possibility. Out there in the Fenlands—drained, inscrutable, rigid, balanced between the real and the mythical—were miles and miles of horizon telling me, with every step, that it was all right to be damaged, hurting, solitary. That they were, too. And that, whether real or imagined, their flattened stretches could hold space for a barely remembered past.

CHAPTER 3

Orford Ness, Shingle Street

بلبل کا بچہ

میں نے اڑایا

واپس نہ آیا

Child of the bulbul: I made him fly, he never came back.

—children's rhyme, 'Bulbul's Child,' 'بلبل کا بچہ'

If you like eerie landscapes, you'll know about Orford Ness: the enigmatic military testing site turned nature reserve in Suffolk. Over the last thirty years, its stark shingle and rusting buildings have become a staple of literature, nature writing and visual art. In all of these works, a motif repeats: the iconic lighthouse, done out in red and white stripes, whose welcoming height stands in counterpoint to the shingle's lovely horizontals.

The Ness reaches out from the Suffolk coast for about ten miles, cut off from the mainland by the River Alde. Its vegetated shingle makes it a rare and special habitat. In England and Wales, we take shingle for granted—about a third of our beaches are shingle—but in fact it's unusual to find it outside northwest Europe, Japan or New Zealand. Vegetated shingle, where plants find ways to survive in the harsh, starved ground, is rarer still. Samphire pokes up from the water like thin, stiff fingers; sea asters and horned poppies patch the shingle with purple and yellow. Among these signs of life, sheep graze. Hares rustle their long ears.

Few people visited the Ness before the twentieth century. It was—still is—only accessible by boat, and what was there to see, once one got there, to make the journey worthwhile? Sheep and shingle: nothing more. This was one of the reasons why the War Department bought part of it in 1913. The already remote Ness became even more distant, closely guarded and enveloped in secrecy. For seventy years, the military experimented on the bare landscape. Camouflage. Aerial photography. Gunsights. Most exciting, to the popular imagination, were whispers about nuclear experimentation and the mysterious 'Cobra Mist' project, begun in 1968. This turns out to be far less interesting than its name suggests: it was a long-range radar system, hampered almost immediately by an unidentifiable noise and shut down five years later. The documented reality tends to be much more prosaic than the setting and the atmosphere.

Orford Ness is treasured culturally as a haunted site. It represents a fantasy of post-apocalyptic space, covered with the contorted remnants of abandoned experiments, now grown over by nature. 'I imagined myself,' W. G. Sebald wrote in *The Rings of Saturn*, 'amidst the remains of our own civilization after its extinction in some future catastrophe.' In such a landscape, everything seems dead and gone. We are relieved from the burden of having to continue living, striving and working. And yet in my experience, when catastrophe actually strikes, it's not like a film: the credits rolling when nothing further can be imagined. Life struggles on, in its small confused way, after everything is over.

When I was fifteen, my father disowned me.

We'd moved house, by this time. We lived away from my grandparents and aunts and uncles. Spot was back from university for the summer. Rabbit was not. That too would prove to be important.

Since my older sisters had left home, there was a little more space. I even had a bookshelf of my own. That day in June, I was sitting on the floor, rearranging my textbooks on the shelf: removing the ones from the O levels I'd just finished to make room for the new ones I'd have as an A-level student. Things were good. With significant hook and crook, I'd found a way to do an English Literature O level. I'd sneaked into the backs of classes, and taught myself one of the texts alone with a study guide, and if my father had noticed the subject on my exam list, he hadn't said anything about it. So I was feeling reckless, and now I had my eye on that A level.

I was happily organizing my books, and Spot was slouched on one arm reading something on the computer, when Forget-Me-Not appeared in the doorway.

'Aba wants you to come to the front room,' she said. Her face was twitching with worry. We never used the front room: its beige brocade sofas were covered over with plastic sheeting, the curtains drawn to protect them from the sun. So this was the first sign something strange was going on. The second was the sight of our aunt and grandmother in the front room, perching on the sofas, looking incongruous.

My father, Spot and I settled next to each other, looking over at my mother, who was hunched in a chair. She'd begun coughing already, bewildered apprehension setting off her asthma.

Slowly and ceremoniously, my father began his speech.

I know everything, he said. You have tried to hide it, but I have found it out.

This is the point where it's almost impossible not to start tracing round the edges of the hole in the middle of the story. The hole which is not the point but which looks like the point, which is understood as the point by everyone I tell it to. But it's a focal point that directs you nowhere, towards nothing.

In Pakistan, gossip keeps people in line. Everyone knows that gossip can send a tense situation suddenly up in flames. Say somebody ripped a page out of the Quran. Or somebody called the prophet a pig. I'm always struck by the detail of these accusations. This is a kind of safety-release valve, I think, for unthinkable thoughts: They are put safely and madly into someone else's mouth, a scapegoat, who's then ritually destroyed. And then the country can close around itself again.

It happened when Rabbit and Spot went to university. Scholarships in western Europe, in the Middle East. The twins were very intelligent, and my father was delighted: he sent them away to study, his girls who were his boys. But this meant that, for the first time, they were out from under his thumb.

In both universities there was a network of Pakistani students. Things could be witnessed, and photographed, and shared.

The incriminating photograph. It's too embarrassing to be real. It's too clichéd. Things only happen like that in books.

And perhaps there were no photographs. All I know of is the rumour of a photograph. I can't even remember who told me. Perhaps the rumour of a photograph would have been enough.

Blackmail. Threats. Shame.

It would have destroyed my father.

The evidence of memory is not admissible.

I am not admissible.

Every crime of this sort needs four witnesses. Four girls in the dock, nudging, whispering, squeezed up close, belted in together, putting their fingertips on the table in front of them for balance.

All the evidence which could be brought in has been deleted, levelled, destroyed. All the parts of my childhood which could have helped me find my bearings are gone. I don't speak enough Urdu. The houses have been demolished. People are dead. Or else not dead enough. Glaring at me, still, whenever I try to speak.

The photograph was not of me. It was nothing to do with me. Everything happened around me, in a fog. But I was near enough to it, pressed up against my sisters as always. That was enough.

We realized that our aunt and grandmother were there as witnesses to an ultimatum. My aunt was glowing. She could hardly keep still. I'd never seen her so pleased.

My father addressed himself to me and Spot. Rabbit was already dead to him. She'd passed beyond the pale. And it was a good thing she'd already run, made her way alone to the UK; she should count herself lucky, he intimated, to be dead only to him.

Equally, it was game over for my mother: She'd betrayed him, by bringing us up so badly. By not telling him the secret, when she must surely have known.

'I didn't know,' she sobbed into her dupatta. 'I didn't know, I had no idea.'

'How could you not have known,' my father scoffed. 'Of course you knew.' He glanced over at us, then repeated, with less certainty but more emphasis: 'Of course you knew.'

Forget-Me-Not would be spared. She was only thirteen—and younger than that, really: young and confused enough to still run over to hug him when he arrived home for a rest in the middle of the day—with pretty pale skin and hair. Almost like a white child, and therefore closer (people thought, without noticing themselves thinking it) to being human. So Forget-Me-Not could go with our mother, if she wanted, but she'd stay my father's daughter, no matter what.

That left two of us. And we had to decide. To live a good Muslim life—stay home, marry as directed—or to get out. 'And you will be dead to me,' he said.

The unnerving thing, in hindsight, was realizing how few narrative options he had. How else might this have gone? What a decision it would have been, to forgive. To accept the choices that had been made. To resist the rush of anger. To brazen it out. It would have been, in fact, an impossible decision. When the small soft part of you is touched, you fold unthinkingly around it.

I don't believe he'd thought much about what would happen after the thrill of the dramatic gesture subsided. When the chips were down, Apollo was of no use to him as a god. Disowning was simply the most convenient response that he found to hand—despite all his past scorn for conservative Pakistani ways—the moment that his omnipotence was threatened. The formula was a familiar one. It gave him a part to perform. He'd ended up playing the Strong Father—and couldn't quite believe it, I think, when we called his bluff. When we chose to be dead.

I first went down to Orford Ness in 2012, on a field trip during my master's. Its bare, flat landscape lifted the hairs on the back of my neck. I'd been transparent as gauze for a while, chilled through in

Cambridge. But something of the trip managed to break through for me. Our tutor gathered us together, spoke about photographs and hauntology and memory, but all my attention was on the horizon over his shoulder. I didn't need the rusting military towers, the bases of the radio masts, to tell me this was a place that had been left as a monument to the end of something.

Most flat landscapes disappear. The water retakes them. Houses accrete upwards over their surfaces. They're ploughed, claimed, conquered, cemented. No one bothers to guard a space which they don't really see, a dead space, a staging ground for their own projects and priorities. Land is at a premium everywhere, especially the flat land which no one loves but everyone wants to use. So it's a particular kind of privilege to be able to come back to a flat place, years after the first visit, and find it still there. In 2021, almost a decade after the trip with my MA group, I visited Orford Ness again. This time, I came armed. I came with friends.

It was October, and too hot: too hot for October and too hot for me, certainly. My friend Rachel picked me up in Peterborough, and we swung towards the coast. Despite our best efforts, it was getting into rush hour. Cars stopped and started, jerking eastwards, as the roads turned sandy underneath us. Above, the sky was pink, mottled with grey-purple clouds. 'They're very Suffolk skies,' my friend said. We drew to a halt in the traffic, and on our right, half under the metal road divider, lay a very small, very perfect baby deer. It was immaculate, its head bent back and its eyes and mouth closed into black lines. Perhaps it had died that same day.

'I know,' Rachel said sadly, when I exclaimed. 'I didn't say anything, I didn't want you to be upset. That happens a lot round here. We'll probably see more as we get closer.'

From then on I was watching, scanning both sides of the road. But I've never been able to understand what I'm looking at when it's moving. It's why I can't drive; grey shapes loom and morph, cobblestones and pavement edges making themselves visible without resolving into spatial sense. So my friend, even with her eyes on the horizon, her mirrors, her dashboard, managed to point out two more deer bodies which I didn't see at all. Worrying, really, to be looking so hard, and not be able to see. What else was I missing?

Other bodies flashed up for me, though: a hedgehog, a pigeon, a pheasant, perhaps a rabbit. Something else, curled up and russet brown. I could guess but didn't want to. Such large and perfect creatures on the pink-brown road. I wanted to stare at their heavy bodies till I understood them. As night closed in, and thick mist lay over the fields with dark trees just surfacing above it, I saw something grey, dismembered, heaped up over the bank; it might have been a deer, or it might have been a sack. In any case, Rachel said nothing when I shouted and twisted, straining to see better, too late.

We reached the village after nightfall. The road was black and the air cool, at last. Gravel crunched and red lights lit the brick-walled turning: our friend Carpenter had arrived already, driven right down from the northeast that day. We welcomed him in whispers, groping through the village, fumbling with the key to push open the front door to our cottage as quietly as we could. Stars shook out over the sky. A satellite inched its way, bit by bit, through the dark.

After my father disowned us, we were given a week to leave. I spent that week floating about, trying not to meet his eye. Everyone moved awkwardly through the space, saying little. There was a box of Mars bars in the fridge in my father's room, cold and hard and bluish. I took them out one by one, and ate them very slowly, one or two a day, and nothing else. Everything had shattered. It was happening at last. The thing I'd daydreamed about for years, but never really believed. We were getting out. It felt like the most cavernous, most exciting loss: everything tipping up and dropping itself into a gaping sea, my friends and my plans and my memories and my home, everything I owned, all pouring down into a deep pale ocean to be left there. Beyond, breathlessly, something wide was opening up, on the other side of this terrifying, balanced week. I could see it. I could almost smell its salt. We just had to get there.

My father was even more unpredictable than usual. One moment, he was giving me a pen to say well done for completing my O levels (I filled it with ink, shook it, tried it out in a scribble on the page: it didn't work). The next, he was screaming at my mother: 'You may think you have won now! But I am of the race of Ibrahaim and I will be avenged!' At one point, he called me into his bedroom and showed me a book he was reading. I stared down at the page, avoiding his eyes, without breathing.

'I am a Sufi, as you well know,' he said. I didn't. 'As you can see here, four levels of enlightenment exist. Most of the people never get beyond level three. Even the great masters. But I have reached level four.'

I nodded, because it had never been more essential to avoid angering him.

In the queue for the Orford bakery—with its pale pink walls and its charming sign, selling Californian bear claws and gibassiers from Provence (I looked them up on my phone), and homemade marshmallows for the hot chocolates—next morning, by a dog that couldn't stop crying, Rachel was fidgeting. She'd spent her holidays in Orford since she was a child.

'Orford's changed so much,' she said. 'This is just a playground for posh Londoners now. When I was little it was a fishing village and no one knew about it.'

The Orford Ness tourist industry had been working full time for a while, drawing money and culture to the village like iron filings to a magnet. The National Trust had sold it well. Everywhere you looked, you saw the remains of a story in the rusting ruins. Now everyone came with money and big cameras to troop around the site and have a haunting, and eat good baking afterwards. And why not? I tucked into my geographically improbable bear claw, sending shattering pastry everywhere, and smiled at Rachel through the sugar.

It wasn't just the bakery that had changed, Rachel said. The famous red-and-white-striped lighthouse had been demolished, only last year. It had stood on the edge of the Ness since 1792. But by 2013, the sea had doggedly eaten its way too far inland, and the lighthouse was decommissioned. Waves lapped at the base of the building. It was time to level it. A crane lifted off the top and lowered it to the ground, with infinite slowness and care. A jackhammer burrowed hopefully into the walls, turning red and white into orange rubble. Why hadn't the lighthouse simply been left to rot with the other ruins on the Ness—the policy of 'managed decline' which lets the military buildings droop and sag in their own time? There were concerns, it seemed, about mercury leaching from the structure into the ecosystem. But perhaps it was also thought wise to slay a symbol of hope swiftly and give the horizon time to get used to it.

From the pictures in our Airbnb, though, you wouldn't have known anything had changed. In the bathroom, a photograph of the lighthouse in rough seas. In the living room, a watercolour sketch of the lighthouse on a bright day, with small pleasure boats sailing near it. The lighthouse was something to photograph, to paint: something for the imagination to organize itself around in this flat space. Too important to give up, even as reality changed under it.

Most landmarks on the Ness lie in ruins, buckled and shrivelled from fifty years of the rain and sun—and yet they are still clearly visible from the village of Orford. Back in the 1950s, the strange huts and towers and pagodas would have been unmissable. The official line given to locals was that the projects were civil, not military, in nature. The employees themselves were almost as much in the dark as everyone else about what truly went on there, fascinated and suspicious about projects in other parts of the site. Even today, the Official Secrets Act restrains former staff from telling everything. And one must tread carefully on the Ness itself. Unexploded ordnance still lurks under the ground. So, of course, the digging never stops. Rumours circulated about charred bodies, flaming seas, plans for biological warfare experiments, foiled Nazi invasions. All the things which make British people squirm with scandalized delight.

'What really happened?' asks one newspaper retrospective after another. 'What really went on?' I'm always interested in which parts of history British people want to know more about, and which parts they're happy to draw a veil over.

In that last week in Pakistan, we found ourselves desperate to hear and tell stories. It was known—gossip again, the fluent workings of the rumour mill—that one of my teachers had left her husband for a while, had lived in the UK, had come back to him. My mother and I went to see her, for advice. I don't know, really, what we wanted, except perhaps for someone to know. We had sworn not to tell anyone: to leave calmly and quietly.

'Does he have a gun?' asked my teacher, when I spilled the whole story to her. Yes, I said. Several. He kept one in his glove compartment, and one under his pillow, and others stashed elsewhere. My mother sat, helpless and terrified, listening. 'Be very, very careful,' my teacher said. 'Make sure the guns stay where they are.' She told us what to do. Consider flying out of a different airport. Peshawar was the one she had used when her husband had tried to section her and take the children. Smile and say nothing until you are close enough to run. Then run. She fled northwest. Take a different road, one he doesn't expect. My mother listened and didn't say that she couldn't drive in Pakistan, was too frightened to tackle its chaotic roads. It was good advice, but we couldn't use it. My teacher didn't tell us why she had come back to her husband, and we didn't ask.

Back at home, we spread photographs over the floors, made piles, made more piles. What will we want to keep? Everything can be replaced except photographs. We snipped out the faces of our aunt. We didn't want to remember her. So some photographs were rectangles and some were squares, with sharp corners poking out.

Twenty kilos of luggage each.

What we couldn't bring were the parrots. Birds have hollow bones, we read on the internet. If you put a bird in a pressurized cabin and take off, the air inside the bones will be a different pressure from outside, and the bird will be crushed. So the birds stayed in Lahore. I said goodbye, then I put them back in their cages, and that was the end. When I left the house I could hear them calling, agitated at all the unfamiliar bustle. I didn't look back. In the end, my father drove us to the airport, and if there was a gun, he kept it in the glove compartment.

When we landed in Britain, we crowded into my maternal grandmother's house. We sat with her and told her how bad things had been. 'Well,' she said comfortingly, after a pause, 'you're here now.' I knew then, and I know now, that I'm not quite here.

Complex PTSD is different from PTSD. It doesn't turn on a single, traumatic event that happened to you. A *single* event. An event that *happened* to you. An event that happened to *you*. It's a story you can't claim as yours. It's the hole in your head.

It's Rabbit's story. She's the main character. It changed everything for me, but it's not mine. What happened to me didn't happen to *me*. I just lived in its terrible air.

When I tell this story, I don't know how to put the emphases in the right places; how to make it matter in the right ways, or not matter in the wrong ways. I tell it flatly, because I don't know how else to tell it. And no one knows what to say. And then I stop.

There's nothing to see here. It's an everyday occurrence. It's less of a story than what happens to most people, most women, in the world. In Britain, every day, if you care to look. It is impossible to narrate this story in any way that makes it matter. If I offered it to you, you'd stare and stare, unsure what you were meant to be looking at.

Supposedly, trauma transcends language and time, and is therefore untellable. Perhaps sometimes it does, and is. But I think traumatized people do know how to tell their stories. What's difficult is that people don't know how to hear them.

What happened on the day my father disowned me offers itself as a focal point in this story where nothing happens. I often tell it like that, and people seize on it gladly. But it isn't an event that matters. It doesn't explain anything. What matters are the fifteen years which came before it. And in those fifteen years, there's nothing which bends into a story.

Next morning, in Orford, we struck out for a walk, round the edge of the village. The boat out to the Ness wasn't until quarter to two, so we had time to case the joint; to circle round and approach slowly, tightening our grip. Over to the left, dark through the heat haze, we could see the main structures on the Ness: two pillared buildings known colloquially as the pagodas. Their low roofs curved upwards at the tips and jutted beyond the pillars that supported them. Peculiar, in this Suffolk village. They claimed the indeterminate bare landscape as something other. The military is its own country: here, it fancied itself a reimagined East Asia.

'That's where they tested detonators,' Rachel said. 'Specially designed, with that shape. If anything went wrong—if they lost control of the explosion—the pillars would blow out and the roof would fall straight down on top of it. Containing it straight away.'

Down below us was a patch of sand, cut through by a channel of water which polished it smooth. I turned off from the path and made my way, carefully, through the little red plants, springy like samphire, over the boggy ground, knowing my friends were watching me with some anxiety. 'And she was never heard from again . . .' I heard Carpenter say behind me. I tested the brown skin of the sand with one foot, but when I gave it my weight my boot sank down with a swift alarming squelch, and beneath the surface the sand was black and smelled of evil. I pulled it out with some effort, and I felt stupid.

At the dock, I was jittery. Getting tickets had required a kind of sorcery. Demand was so high that the National Trust released batches of new tickets every two weeks, to be snapped up by hungry daytrippers within hours. I'd called and called all summer, trying to prebook; I knew the names of Alastair and Seb and Naomi at the Orford Ness office. Now we were waiting for Naomi, who was going to take us out with her. At least, that was the plan. I didn't trust it. I hadn't heard from Naomi in weeks. What if they turned us away? What if the booking had been lost or misrecorded? At the front of the queue, I introduced myself nervously.

'Oh, you're Noreen. Yes. I'm Naomi.'

I stared at her calm, lean face, perhaps fifty; at the lizard pin and rainbow National Trust badge on her lanyard.

'Yes, that's all fine. Just wait outside. I'll lock up the office, but don't panic when you see the blinds come down, I'm not going anywhere, and in a while I'll be out and we'll all go.'

For something to do, I bought an Orford Ness pin from the little blue cardboard tray and attached it to my T-shirt. It was round, framing one of the pagodas dramatically against an orange sky, a blue river winding away from it. Green lines shot towards the pagoda, like a fussily cultured ornamental garden. It was meant, I thought, to evoke a kind of pan-Oriental scene.

We waited, by the anti-smuggling sign that said BOATS ARRIVING AT UNUSUAL TIMES? and after a while Naomi joined us and led us down to the quay, where the boat was just drawing in, by the splayed union flag and the memorial stone. FROM THIS QUAY FOR OVER 70 YEARS MEN & WOMEN CROSSED THE RIVER ORE TO SERVE THEIR COUNTRY.

On the crossing I found that I couldn't really take my eyes off Naomi. I drew in my knees and tried to look organized, but she hadn't noticed me. When we reached the Ness, she disembarked, said goodbye to the skipper and strode calmly off into the distance with a mop. I watched her go.

A volunteer instructed us in the three different trails—blue, red and green—that we could choose from. One had to follow the established routes. It was absolutely forbidden to stray off the paths: not only was there a risk of unexploded ordnance waiting in the shingle beyond, but careless boots might disturb fragile ecosystems. We could choose any of those three colour-coded routes to explore. I put up my hand.

'Which is the flattest?'

'They're all flat!'

Everybody laughed. I didn't.

A piece of crossed wood stuck out from the river, perhaps a weathered signpost, like a crucified Christ with wide wings.

Along the road we came to a green van and a man named Ken, who stood up as we approached. I gave my name and he wrote down MATHMOOD X 3 in big letters, and directed us to the red route. Stony District, Rangers Office, Bomb Ballistics Building, Back Beacon, AWRE Laboratory 1. I fell behind, as my friends drew generously ahead, and looked down at the grey road, spotted with pieces of mud. The banks were striped with yellow and green grass, brushed sideways and upwards by a fussy, indecisive wind. Up ahead was a wide channel of water, a pale grey-blue which matched the lowest part of the sky. When you sent your gaze further up, it rose into a deeper and deeper blue.

To my right, in the brown ground, were pools of water catching the sun. Like silver coins; like buffalo pools. Instead of buffalo heads, peering neck deep out at the world, grass stood up from the surface, each blade dark and distinct as beard stubble. Nearby was a long, thin patch of flattened grass, pale at the edges and crossed like a ladder with stem shadows, as though something long had lain down for a while, then got up and walked away. The grass lay at every angle, sending my eyes in all directions at once, making me feel floaty. But I couldn't float too far. The line of the horizon gave me a ceiling, kept me at a level: I let myself rise right up to it, lost in the lines of a landscape which kept me busy looking, which wouldn't let my vision go.

Strange things come into your mind as you walk in a flat landscape. What came to me then, pacing along the trail, was Elizabeth Bishop's urgent, mysterious poem 'Chemin de Fer,' about quite another landscape:

> Alone on the railroad track
> I walked with pounding heart.
> The ties were too close together
> or maybe too far apart.

The scenery was impoverished:
scrub-pine and oak; beyond
its mingled gray-green foliage
I saw the little pond

where the dirty hermit lives,
lie like an old tear
holding onto its injuries
lucidly year after year.

The hermit shot off his shot-gun
and the tree by his cabin shook.
Over the pond went a ripple.
The pet hen went chook-chook.

'Love should be put into action!'
screamed the old hermit.
Across the pond an echo
tried and tried to confirm it.

The pounding heart, the ties, the lonely railroad track. I don't know where the poem is set—probably Bishop's birthplace, Massachusetts—but I recognized the feeling. The hot, still path underfoot, on the brink of meaning something, drawing me urgently along towards something that didn't seem to be there. An imperceptible distress in the landscape that you can't pin down. The poet's mind rearranges the landscape anxiously, trying to find a solution: Should the ties be closer together? Farther apart? And at the end of the poem, an echo trying and failing to materialize. It should be there but isn't.

Behind me, I could hear a group of people discussing the way the cuckoo lays its eggs. In another bird's nest, of course: the baby cuckoo hatches, and shoulders the other eggs, the other nestlings, over the side and out, until there is just one huge baby cuckoo and two tiny bewildered parents, feeding it endlessly.

I was feeling dissociated. I didn't know why. Everything I needed was here—the sun was out, the land was spread before me—but I couldn't feel good in it or with it. I was feeling very little. I didn't know what I needed from the landscape, or what it needed from me.

Ahead, my friends turned into one of the Ness's museum buildings. I followed them, glancing at the boards with their diagrams of missile trajectories, and whispered into their ears: some kind of excuse, going to take the air, whatever it was. At the same time, I was trying to keep myself turned away, a little, from them. Why should they have to bear it, after all? Why should they have to bear me? My hot skin, my hot breath, my sweat, my strange prickly living presence?

I took myself outside again to wait.

I sat down on the grass, by a large metal cube distorted by rust and full of weeds like a gigantic planter. Ahead of me, a pylon had leaned right over, by forty-five degrees. The air was warm on my face and neck. October. I could hear the grasshoppers buzzing around me, could see brambles spilling out of their planter, still ripe for the taking. I was wearing a T-shirt and shorts. Soon climate change would blister the metal remains of the buildings away to nothing, I thought, and I was tired of the thought even before I'd finished thinking it.

I turned my gaze towards a still, shaded tree, and my head filled with the first lines of Wallace Stevens's 'The Dwarf':

Now it is September and the web is woven.
The web is woven and you have to wear it.

There's a danger in the autumn that Stevens and Bishop knew about. Something terrible is about to happen, contained in a loveliness so intense and precarious, a beauty that could tip over at any moment into terror. Ground deeply into this beauty is a grimness, a resignation. The web is woven. The track is laid. You have to bear it.

I knew I was seeing Orford Ness through too many pairs of eyes already. I was in someone else's ready-made story. People are drawn to Orford Ness because the ruins suggest stories. The fragments are like a dot-to-dot; brains leap instantly to join them up. It's the Gestalt theory of perception. Given only a few disconnected traces on a page, we automatically fill in the missing parts, and see the shape which we've been culturally primed to perceive.

The story Orford Ness suggests is about war, and that's what made it matter. In war, there's tension, two opposing sides, a winner and a loser. Violence and conquest. Facts and strategies and evidence. And war is a male story, which makes it automatically legible to other people.

One of the few things my father never bragged about was how he'd fought in the 1971 war between Pakistan and Bangladesh. The two used to be one country: West Pakistan and East Pakistan. East Pakistan had the larger population, but West Pakistan held all the power from the moment the country split off from India. In 1971, East Pakistan called for self-determination, and West Pakistan cracked down brutally. India waded in. The war lasted thirteen days. About three million people died. West Pakistani soldiers raped hundreds of thousands of girls and women, and millions more fled over the border to India.

My father was seventeen when the war broke out. Underage, he signed up to fight, illegally. His best friend was blown up next to him. A bullet passed through his hand, which still bore a puckered scar on the palm.

That's all I know. As I say, he never talked about it.

War and whiteness organize the world. They tell you what you can imagine and what you can't: what stories you can revel in and what stories get burnt up into feathers of ash and taken away by the wind. Only the war stories of white people seem to matter. They offer a line through: a beginning and an end.

Orford Ness: whiteness and war. The trails you must not stray from, for fear of being blown up. No matter how you try, it's impossible to write any totally new story. Your mind bends back and down the paths carved out for it. You find yourself, always, telling a story you already know. You register it, like a rubber stamp coming down, and you move on.

We tell stories to make them visible. Or we tell stories so that we don't have to look at them any longer.

And all the ready-made trails, into which my story threatened to fall, were wrong. I didn't want to tell the story on which the right-wing press pounced gleefully, about Pakistan being evil, or Pakistanis, or Muslims, or even my father. Nor the story about triumphing over adversity. Mine didn't seem to be any sort of story at all. Just some things that didn't happen, or that happened to someone else.

Then I spotted a grasshopper. It was making its way—half jumping, half blown—over the grey tarmac. I filmed it. What would come out, when I watched it back later, was no grasshopper, but only an indistinct movement: something which might be a blowing, or a shaking in me and my hands.

I turned round, then, and my friend Rachel was behind me, very quiet and gentle. I jumped up, and as I did I saw the lower jaw of a rabbit half buried in the moss. Rachel waited for me, saying nothing, as I dug around it with my fingers. The bone had gone soft; it fell apart like wet paper, and I left it there.

The rabbit bone had helped: I started to feel a little better. At least, I decided to try to. My shadow stretched ahead of me in the dangerous sun; a dragonfly tucked its tail under and spun in midair. People overtook me as I dawdled. 'Brian's sister, Karen, has got all the . . .' If you liked ruins, there was plenty to see: the remnants of a brick structure with two stubs of broken toilet sticking up out of it. Side by side, as though two friends might have sat on them together, chatting. Ahead was a tree covered, strangely, in what looked like white blossoms. This made no sense. Behind it, streaks of pale cloud shot upwards. I stared at them and they rearranged themselves, resolving into tall, thin pylons, or towers of wire, white against the purple-grey sky.

What startled me most on the Ness was the colour. The red on the ground; the yellow stalks of strange flowers I couldn't name; the scaly orange of a tree in the grip of lichen to the farthest tips of its branches; the green and tawny gold of the grasses, with the dry, brown skeletons of tall, stiff plants poking through. The yellow grass had a sheen; it looked soft and it trembled in my vision, which changed planes again and again to accommodate it. Snail shells were smashed open by the side of the path. I picked one up and wore it on my finger. As I came towards the bridge—my friends already clattering across it—the red-gold vegetation surrounded me, dotted with pools like shapes cut out of red felt.

But it wasn't until I followed my friends out on to the shingle that I felt my mouth open to hang as I looked out. The beach was almost white in the afternoon sun, with teasels stuck up like cacti: their jaunty arms coming out both ways, wearing their spiky heads like big gloves. I closed my hand around one clenched teasel fist, and it hurt me. Against the bright sky, they were cut as sharply as the long shadows of grass on the ground. I was back in my body with my hand around a teasel, which was doing its job, spiky and frizzed, doing just what was needed, as all things do.

I caught up with my friends and walked beside them, saying nothing. We came to a white building, battered by the wind and sea for years, until now the streaky orange wood showed through. A ladder ran up the side; if you climbed it, you could reach a kind of balcony above, where people were milling around with binoculars. A viewpoint, then, from which one could look out over the Ness. But I was tired, and I didn't care. I didn't want to be steered up and down by what other people were doing, along the tracks their feet were making in the world. Also, there was a strange buzzing coming from somewhere in the building, which seemed more interesting. It was like a sound of something wrong: something which wasn't meant to be there.

I left my friends and wandered round to find a doorway, a room held up by tall grey columns. There were large orange outlines on the walls, where metal shapes had been pulled off by force, taking the plaster with them. The buzzing grew louder as I approached, and I saw a pile of twigs and leaves at the back of the room. I felt an awful prickle of dread, as though I knew what I'd find. Standing over it, the sound was deafening. But I couldn't see anything: no insects—no abject object of horror—on which they might have been clustering. There was nothing there at all.

I turned my back on it firmly and left, returning to my friends waiting outside.

As we walked on, the sound of the shingle changed and deepened: its crunch was lower underfoot, something more structural. But the path onwards was abruptly barred off. A sign apologized. Access to the beach had been restricted, for security reasons. It echoed all the other signs across the Ness—now mostly defunct—warning of military operations as moss grew in their cracks and their wood turned soft. But this one was much newer, modern, and I realized why when Rachel pointed out at the horizon.

'There,' she said. 'That's where the lighthouse was.' A double pile of rubble and something like a house off to the right. There was no longer anything to see here. No longer any God, any shape of God, to see and to help and to guide. Just some scattered structures, engaged in making their way vaguely back down to the ground they'd been built on.

I lifted a rusty curve of metal, like half a shackle, from the side of the path. What had it been? It was small enough for me to put in my bag, like a piece of shingle, to carry away with me. But then, I knew, it would stop meaning anything. It would be a bit of inert rubbish. I put it back. Green grass made its way on to the path, escaping the pale yellow grass on either side, staining the bare rubble.

As we moved on, the horizon stayed the same. What moved under it was the grass: now lying in straight lines, like waves or tidal dunes, now swerving in patchy curves. But it grew barer and barer, and darker, until, for brief and precious moments, the only thing visible was the land itself, its shingled rises and falls flattened into a curtain by the horizon. In that light, it was the colour of the sandy bare banks of the Ravi. I started at the thought. The river which flowed by Lahore was often dried up to hardly more than a trickle. There was a picture of me, somewhere, as a tiny child, squatting in a colourful jumper and orange trousers—so it must have been wintertime—playing on my own in that grey sand. In the corner of the photograph, unknown men stood and watched.

And now the pagodas were getting closer, peering up at us over the shingle. But a screech of an electric bike made me look round. It was a volunteer ranger in a green shirt.

'Sorry, you've got to start turning back! You're already well late for the last boat!' He said 'well late' with great emphasis, as though he was very pleased.

Of course, we were not. But we went back anyway. There was no sign of Naomi as we left the Ness behind.

That night I drank half a glass of white wine, leaving the glass cloudy and fingerprinted on its coaster, and I told my friends—for the first time—about why we'd left Pakistan. I thought they knew already. I thought everyone knew. But they didn't. We'd known each other all this time, and still. So I told it to them, as well as I could, as well as I've done here, or maybe a little better. And at the end I asked: 'Is it a story?' The tears started to drip. 'I never know whether it's a story.'

They were hugging me. I couldn't explain what I meant.

Next morning we went out on the River Ore, on a boat called the *Lady Flo*. Inside the cabin, I spotted the lost lighthouse again, in a painting by the big bell. Sun turned to drizzle, and I was pleased; it would have felt odd to see this landscape only in idyllic sunlight. One needs the cloud and the dark sky, the shiver and the trickle, or at least I do. The boat circled the Ness, and the landscape we'd walked yesterday slid by at quite another angle. From here, the tall towers were black, not white. As the boat moved, they collapsed into a line like a pack of cards, then fanned out again. The land thinned out into a strip of darkness, and a digger scooped slowly away by itself.

The *Lady Flo*'s tour guide narrated the various landmarks as we passed. The pagodas. The tower which broadcast BBC radio. The 'Black Beacon,' used for radio navigation in the thirties. We'd seen them all and now we were seeing them again. But I sat right up and craned my neck when the guide pointed out the 'Chinese Wall.' This seawall had been built by a Chinese labour battalion, he told us, before the boat moved on and so did he. I filed the knowledge mentally, and when I got home later, I looked it up. The Chinese labour battalions were groups of Chinese people who entered the First World War on the side of the Allies: largely forgotten and omitted from many histories of the conflict. I'd certainly never heard about them before. They didn't fight, but they dug trenches, built walls and barracks, unloaded military supplies, to release British and French men to serve on the front line. The figures vary: it could have been anything between 140,000 and 320,000 Chinese people working behind the scenes in this way. Most of those recruited were from very poor areas in China, attracted by the food, clothing and family support on offer. The journey to Europe was dangerous, and once there the labour battalions had to contend with unexploded ammunition, enemy fire, illness and a harsh climate. And now their contribution to the war is almost completely forgotten. Britain was very unwilling to acknowledge the presence and role of Chinese labour in its war, and China didn't want Germany to know it had cooperated. The men themselves were largely illiterate; few were able to leave detailed diaries or accounts of what had happened to them. In a telling sequence of events, a gigantic cyclorama called the *Panthéon de la Guerre*, erected in Paris as a monument to the war, originally included Chinese labourers among its figures—but these were painted out to make room for US soldiers, when the latter country joined the war. I think there is a reluctance, in Britain, to acknowledge the fact that the First World War looked very ethnically different from the all-white panoramas which nourish Remembrance Sundays and wartime memorials. At Orford Ness, the Chinese Wall still quietly keeps the sea back, while the pseudo-Chinese 'pagodas,' designed by the West for military testing, tower above it.

In the end, I found, I had little to say to the Ness. There was too much ruin there. And it had been written over, again and again, by other people: their versions, accounts, memories. White male memory, mostly. Bombs and drama, with no space for anyone or anything that might matter to me. I had nothing to add.

But on the last morning of our stay, as we were packing up to leave and sweeping breadcrumbs into the bin bag, Rachel said: 'I really think we should go by Shingle Street on the way back. It's out of our way, a little. But I think you'll find it useful.'

'What's Shingle Street?'

'It's another sort of stretch of shingle. Quite like the other side of the Ness: the bit we didn't get to, before we got turned back. It's very flat. I think you'll like it.'

The car turned one way, then another, down country roads, bursting occasionally into the dazzling Suffolk sky, with gathered dots of trees. Gauzy light streaked overhead, brushed with blue as from a caught sleeve. We drew up at a car park, backed by ordinary yellow fields, white railings, an unsteady fringe of horizon. And in front of us—towards the sea—

<u>THIS IS NOT A CAR PARK</u>
The Land Owners accept <u>NO</u> responsibility
for the loss of property or damage to vehicles
on this site. There is **no vehicle access** to
and beyond the concrete ramps.

Welcome to Shingle Street. A sign with a red circle and a white horizontal line; behind it, a white sky and a horizontal line of no colour. Bare twigs curved and pointed up, towards the clouds. The landscape lined up, against itself. All I could see was shingle, rising in a great wall, bare as sand.

Off to the left was one house, drawn tactfully back from that skyline. And a couple of walkers, silhouetted like little ruffled crows. I wanted to shout and cry. Swallow it, in a gulp of air.

We got out on the shingle and faced the sun. From there, pockmarked toffee-brown rubble filled the whole horizon. Patches of grass embossed it, like luxurious circles of embroidery: green, purple-green, yellow. Nothing moved. There was as much space as anyone could want. It was the purest flatness I'd ever stood in.

Rachel set out into the shingle. I watched her go. In her pale blue fleece, her form marked, even more deeply, the space there, her shadow stretching behind. After a moment, I followed, my feet sliding and scrabbling with a wet crunch. My mind seemed to throb up and down, into the sky, out of sync with what my feet were doing. The land looked flat, but somehow as I walked I found that I was being carried up and over—a ridge or a swell that perspective had hidden from me—and there opened up between the sky and the shingle a pale band of sea, a darker band of shingle beyond. The physics made no sense to me. This flatland could fold inclines and valleys into itself, and still be—still feel—perfectly flat. It was a miracle I accepted without trouble. Over in the distance, grass patches receded from view, like small unhurried turtles making their way home. Staring out to the horizon, I felt as though I could be in a desert, the sun breaking through the clouds, giving texture and shadow to the shingle. Then I turned a hundred and eighty degrees: there, quite simply, was the ordinary English countryside, a house, a row of terraced houses. Something had split the world here. Something had broken in.

As we crunched over this strange desert, we came to a dip and—in it—a lake. Chilled silver by the pale sky, it was fluttering at the edges. The ground curved down smoothly to meet the horseshoe of water, like an Italian almond horn biscuit cut out of the shingle.

I looked round at the lone house again and imagined living there. Waking up every morning to stare out across the flatness, the shimmering sea. Not heaven: heaven is when things are done for good. This would be a life quickened into interest and enquiry and presence, daily, every moment of the day, by a landscape which could draw out—for miles—the spirit in you.

'I remember they made a work of art on this beach.' Rachel had come up next to me. She was holding a little pile of oyster shells between thumb and finger, stacked like saucers. 'A woman with cancer, I think it was. A long line of shells.'

We didn't see the 'Shell Line' that day, but I looked it up, much later. It was made by Lida Kindersley and her friend Els Bottema, both from the Netherlands. Lida was diagnosed with cancer. Two months later, so was Els.

'It's not okay,' Lida says, in the documentary *C Shells*.

'No, no,' Els agrees. 'It was not okay.'

She remembers: 'And then . . . Lida said, Hey Els, you know what, when we're through all these therapies of all kinds, I know a place where we can recover, where we can meet and try to—'

'Begin life again, really, wasn't it,' Lida supplies.

In Shingle Street, they could be together, just quietly, or talk about what they'd been through. And walk, as little or as much as they could manage. Els gathered white whelk shells in her pocket. One morning, together, they started putting those shells down on the shingle. After that, they came back every six months, and every time they added more shells to the line. 'Only the whelks, the white whelks,' they write in their book *The Shingle Street Shell Line* (2018). Grey whelks may be gathered in caches, the white line looped around them. No cowries or limpets. Now the line's about three hundred yards long, as long as it can be, because the sea ends it.

less flexible now, we lay the shells
  line-repair now, as it can be of no greater length
    it is complete and yet never done, never

In the film, the two women lie on the shingle, propped up on their elbows—grey-haired, middle-aged, in big coats—and fit white whelk shells, most with gaping holes in their broadest whorls, into gaps in the line.

'Of course they're all a bit broken,' one says, in the film. 'We're all a bit broken.'

I was happy that the shell line was there. Like a white scar, like an incision. I liked the idea that women had, quietly, made something on a flat space together.

And I was happy, also, that I hadn't seen it.

That day on the shoreline, the sea made a scooped pattern, a scalloped edge in the shingle. I picked up a stone, then another, then— my heart thumped—a hagstone. Hagstones, traditionally, are magic, with a hole worn through by water. Look through the hole and you can see fairyland. Or you can tie them to the bedpost to ensure fertility. Or wear them for luck and protection. Everyone loves a hagstone, and they seem to do everything, all the magic you could imagine, depending on who you ask. Robert Macfarlane and Stanley Donwood used them as chapter dividers in their prose-poem *Ness*, and gave them to one character for eyes. But this hagstone had another little stone wedged in its hole: the same fudge-brown colour, but shot with grey. I pushed, first with my thumbnail, then with a sharp-cornered rock, but it wouldn't budge. The way through had been blocked. When I held up the hagstone, lining the stopper there was only a crescent of light.

I took it home, anyway. And over time I loved it more and more. Later, I would tie another hagstone on a friend's bedpost: Rachel, who walked with me in Shingle Street that day, to give her luck and—we hoped—a baby. That was an ordinary, clean hagstone I picked up on Tynemouth beach, smooth and sandy-coloured; I guess you could see fairyland clear in that stone, if you wanted. But I kept the one from Shingle Street. It was proof of something thwarted. Stopped in its tracks. A thing held, but not ever seen. A way through that is no way through.

In Greek drama, catastrophe is the event that happens right before the end. Everything that follows is just tidying up, conclusion. *Cata* suggests downwards, but also: thoroughly, completely. Catastrophe comes from the Greek καταστροφή: an overturning, a sudden turn, a downturn.

When the great turn happened in my life, when the catastrophe came for us, it was deceptive. It didn't manage to bring on the end of everything. Though everything in its wake feels, and may always feel, like a tidying-up after it.

It didn't feel like a downturn. It felt like becoming weightless, rising up.

Death goes on pulsing, growing, fading and reappearing, crawling up out of the sea. What I do know is this. The thing which didn't happen to me was meant to be catastrophic. It was meant to annihilate us from the story. But my life started there, in the wake of what I remember experiencing—in amongst everything, the parrots and the photographs and the gun—as vertiginous hope.

In Suffolk, I picked through the shingle with the toes of my boots. In that space, everything spilled over past its own ending, just like I was doing in my own life simply by being alive. Nothing was hidden. Not even the bony, silent woman—unaccountably, improbably still here, still going—making her way across the flat expanse.

CHAPTER 4

Morecambe Bay

> . . . the constant presence and threat of trauma in the
> lives of girls and women of all colors, men of color . . .
> lesbian and gay people, people in poverty and people
> with disabilities has shaped our society, a continuing
> background noise rather than an unusual event.
> —Laura S. Brown, 'Not Outside the Range: One
> Feminist Perspective on Psychic Trauma'

The flat place is the place of grief, but also the place of the real. It's real because of that grief: it displays itself starkly, and you are beside yourself in the face of what can't be denied. But at least you are beside yourself. You have that consolation. You curl your fingers into a fist and pretend you are holding a hand.

I've met people before, in the flat place. Once in a while I'll encounter someone—and you can recognize them quite quickly, it spills out of their eyes and their closed mouths, even when they're smiling—whose world's been rolled out on the rack in the same way as mine. And I fall in love with them, usually, because they feel real to me in a way no one else does. In that flat place where no one else can come, we crouch together, holding each other tight, feeling what is real thrum underfoot and the sky run over our heads. And my blood beating in their head, and the other way round. But always, in the end, we part, walking away over a landscape in which one is always alone.

It's no good, relating to someone else like that. The psychological term for it is merging. To me, it feels like I don't exist anymore. I feel as though I become a room in which the other person lives. I become the breath in their lungs which Margaret Atwood called 'that unnoticed / & that necessary' in her poem 'Variation on the Word *Sleep*.' It's intoxicating, and it's devastating. But I don't know any other way to be. I don't know what love looks like, if it's not a kind of vanishing.

Relationships are one of the most challenging aspects of complex PTSD. They're both the source of terror and the cure for that terror. The psychoanalyst Robert Stolorow argues that trauma is the loss of attachment to other people. Complex PTSD develops in part when one doesn't have functioning responsive attachments: when the attachment figures fail to protect one from a frightening world, or—more often—when they are that frightening world. The baby doesn't learn to experience other people as a source of safety. It doesn't learn to attach.

So the way to start repairing from cPTSD is to create healthy attachments, to feel connected to others and safe with them.

'What does it feel like?' I asked my therapist. 'To feel connected to another person?'

She smiled at me, helplessly. I knew I was asking her to do something impossible. Like describing *red* to someone who's never seen colour. Without those early experiences of feeling totally held and safe, I didn't know how to be in relationship to another person without tensing up or disappearing mentally from the situation. But if I didn't know how it was supposed to feel, how would I know if I was feeling it?

'Really connected, I mean,' I said. 'In a good way. Where there's room for both of us, and we're both real.'

It sounded, to me, like I was describing a paradox. How could the sun and the moon be in the sky simultaneously? How could two people be present to each other at the same time?

'Like,' I said, 'are you here with me, now?'

'Yes,' my therapist said. 'I'm here with you. But *I'm* also here. Even when I'm paying full attention to you, listening carefully to everything you say, a little part of my mind is also aware—let's say— of my leg, or my hand. And that's good. It keeps *me* here, with you.'

My life only has two layers. On the top is thick joy, moving around like the sea, full of fish and slopping goofily at the edges: active and exuberant and amazed by everything. The bottom layer is the cold sea floor, where insects pick through dead things. I'm in the top layer, and then suddenly I'm tired and I'm back on the floor, my cheek against the whisper that says nothing matters.

There's no space in between.

It's been shown that preexisting healthy relationships can head off trauma, can prevent distressing events from developing into PTSD. A five-year-old who witnessed the plane crashing into the Twin Towers ran out of his classroom and downstairs straight into his parents' arms. He didn't develop PTSD for two reasons: he was able to take an active role by running away from it, and he was able to join his loving, connected parents, with whom he felt safe.

Touch is a key part of that connection. When asked how he treats acute trauma, one psychiatrist recommends, 'Holding them, rocking them, giving them massages, calming their bodies down.' When I first read about this technique, I felt a lump in my throat. It reminded me of when I was twenty-seven and my then partner took me to see the Hardy Tree in London. The story goes that when Thomas Hardy worked there, exhuming graves and clearing gravestones, he placed all the extra gravestones in overlapping circles around this particular tree. In the evening light, the tree shot up from the stones clustering around it. They were like souls, like children, tugging at its skirts, moaning for attention. The tree arched away from them but couldn't escape. And the gravestones were pressed together, skin to skin, for all eternity. It was the worst thing I had ever seen, and I almost cried.

My partner couldn't understand. 'I think it's lovely. They're not alone. They get to be close to each other, forever.'

The thought made me sick. To be immobilized forever by other bodies. Touch is complicated for me because it repulses me even as I crave it. I can't think, I can't feel, when there's another person against me. I love to hug and to touch, but I am not there while it's happening.

But after I read about holding and rocking as a treatment for trauma, the idea of being rocked became a fantasy I returned to. When I was tired, as I always was, I climbed into bed and closed my eyes and told myself a story about being held close to someone. And yet I knew if anyone tried to do that to me, I would be possessed by anxiety. I'd be tense in their arms, trying to work out if they were growing tired, monitoring them for signs of ambivalence or disgust. Perhaps they would be offended by my smell. Perhaps my weight would crush them.

Above all, I had the image of someone putting their hands on my stomach. My stomach which cramped, kicked, dissolved, swelled; which held everything in my life that I didn't understand; which tried to do everything to break away from me. If someone put their hands on my stomach, I thought, I would be able to feel its outlines at last; I'd know where it began and ended. Lying with lovers, cold in all the places I was meant to feel something, having done (I hoped) more or less the right things with my face and voice—enough to stop them from asking me what was wrong—I dared to move their hands to my stomach. After a moment, they always moved them away, like changing the subject when a conversation gets awkward. So there was something strange, I thought, about my stomach. No one wanted it. It seemed more private and dangerous than anything else my lovers touched freely. I put my own hands on it, but the doubleness of the sensation confused me: I could feel my stomach on my hands, as well as my hands on my stomach. I took my hands away again.

So I needed other people, to find my own shape. And I loved people too: I adored my friends, with a kind of fannish disbelief that they allowed me in their presence. But being with them could be unbearable. I was always on my guard, unable to relax fully. Either I went into their worlds, or I stayed in mine. We didn't seem to be able to build a world together, a common landscape.

'What would it look like, to bring people into your world?' asked my therapist.

At Morecambe Bay, in northwest England, mudflats stretch for miles, cut through by the River Kent, spread over with samphire. Oystercatchers pick their way through the landscape, clustering protectively in groups. In the sky, low ribboned clouds let through stripes of dazzle, glittering on the wet sand. The poet Norman Nicholson described crossing the bay, in 1955, as an entrance into a 'strange kingdom,' transformed, between one side of the bay and the other, in its people, its language, its very substance: 'an amphibian world that was neither earth nor water, and when at last [the walker] emerged from the sands and mists and mosses . . . the people spoke a dialect harder to understand for some than French or Italian.' Might this dreamy amphibian world change things, somehow, for me?

But the serene landscape is also treacherous. Quicksand can take an unsuspecting walker, or even a hapless vehicle; tides come in rapidly. For centuries, anyone wanting to walk across the bay has had to be accompanied by a special guide. The King's (or Queen's) Guide to the Sands is usually a local fisherman with knowledge of the area. Once a fortnight, in the summer, the guide leads groups, sometimes numbering hundreds, on the eight-mile Cross Bay Walk. There is no exact route for this walk—it depends on the wind and the tide—and therefore it cannot be mapped. To cross this land, you have to put your trust in other people.

This flatland walk sounded unbearable. No solitude, no control. I decided to do it.

The summer trips get booked out fast by organizations hoping to fundraise. Hearing Dogs, Cumbria Community Foundation, Galloway's Society for the Blind . . . I signed up to their waiting lists, and crossed my fingers, because the only date with definite vacancies was the walk commandeered by the British Naturist Society. Walking naked, in a crowd of people, was—I thought—an inexcusably potent metaphor. And it would be distracting. And the straps of my backpack would chafe. But I told all my friends about it anyway, because it was a story, and we laughed.

I scrolled through the photos of earlier trips. A group of older women, smiling in Motor Neurone Disease Association T-shirts. Tourists in very smart sunglasses and visors, fiddling with their cameras. Families with children, arguing animatedly as their dads brushed sun cream onto the backs of their arms.

Children. Even the thought made me tense. There would definitely be children, and they would run around, fight, scream. Worst of all, they might try to make friends with me. I didn't want to touch or talk to any children. They were hot, damp, needy. I flinched when they were noisy; I flinched when their parents shouted. If I ever saw a child being hit, I could feel the fear and the rage in strange places in my body: stiffening up my arm, crowding into my face and lips. And at the same time, whatever they did, I heard a small savage voice in my head: *horrible little bastards; I'd like to give them a good kick, make them shut up, learn how to behave.* That corner of my mind was the last remaining stronghold of my father's voice. It was frightening to hear, especially from myself. I didn't like overhearing myself hating the hot, damp, needy, frightened little girl I used to be.

But I would be fine on Morecambe Bay. It was easy to feel alone in a crowd. It might even be interesting to eavesdrop, to watch how everyone else reacted to the wide horizons, the glistening flats, the colossal sky.

As long as no one dared to speak to me.

At Newcastle, we stood waiting to board a grubby Northern train with four carriages. I wasn't enjoying this 'we.' It was mostly loud men. My legs were hurting and agitated. The train could not leave the station because, as it turned out, a headless pigeon corpse was blocking the mechanism where the two carriages connected. Eventually, a member of the train crew put in his finger and thumb and pulled first a pigeon wing, then a pigeon body, bent against it like a concertina, out of the train's innards and onto the track. The crew member wiped his bare hands shudderingly against each other and hauled himself back into the carriage. The doors opened, and we boarded and rode away, leaving the dead bird behind us.

This was, I realized, one of the only times in my life I'd travelled west across the UK. An unknown sensation. Travelling south was the worst: it felt yellow, a low deep roar getting louder and louder, like insects circling and the air thickening and something very dangerous waking up. Travelling east wasn't as bad. It was a shrivelling, a going-pale. But the only safe way to move was north, where things darkened and gathered in, and the fresh cold blew, and a long winter held you as you waited things out. Travelling west was new, and I prepared to see how it would feel. Prudhoe, Hexham, Haltwhistle. Carlisle: City of the Lakes. The rain drove down, and I closed my eyes against the mountains of the Lake District and lay back in my seat.

Every country is built on some idea of a 'we': a maths of belonging and not-belonging. Pakistan's 'we' seemed, on one level, very simple. It was founded on the basis of religion. It would be a Muslim country. A place where Indian Muslims could find belonging and safety from oppression by the Hindu majority. When India campaigned for independence from the British Empire in the early twentieth century, a set of Muslim voices spoke up for a Muslim homeland carved out, at the same time, from India's vast territory. They were led by Muhammad Ali Jinnah: a gaunt, finicky, Westernized man in fine suits, who—I gathered, from his image on banknotes and in my school textbooks—looked not unlike my own father.

So in 1947, four Muslim-majority areas in the West of India— West Punjab, Sindh, Balochistan and the North-West Frontier Province—joined with East Bengal, 1,500 kilometres away, to become Pakistan, at the same time as the rest of India gained independence from the British. But immediately the country was faced with the question: What did it actually mean to be Pakistani? What, in practise, is a 'Muslim homeland'? Jinnah was no help. He crumpled and died of tuberculosis a year later, and the country was left to work things out on its own.

Since then, the question hasn't really been resolved. Is it a homeland for all Muslims? Just for Muslims from India? Just for Muslims in the provinces chosen to join Pakistan? And who counts as a Muslim, anyway? All sects, practises, interpretations—or a single, official version of the faith? Should Pakistan's laws be secular or shaped by sharia? In the absence of concrete answers, modern Pakistan is constructed on acts of exclusion which are both extremely strict and extremely vague. Its instability, its coups, its wars, its various violences, derive in many ways from the fact that *no one can feel, with confidence, that they belong in Pakistan.*

It was no wonder, really, that I had no sense of how to connect with other people. Stuck in its own postcolonial drift, Pakistan had never been able to work out, either, what it meant to belong.

At the hotel in Carnforth, there was an incident.

I'd collected my key and found my corridor, passing a heterosexual couple on the way who were talking and laughing, his arm slung round her shoulders. I padded along the dull pink carpet towards my room, and then it reached me. A smell. In an instant my whole body was ice. I knew that smell. A man's hair—shampoo, a specific brand, and something deeper, bodily, pheromonal. I was in a room I couldn't see, at a time I couldn't pin down, with a person I couldn't identify. My teeth were clenched, and inside me something was flapping in panic.

I stopped and half fell over, one hand reaching out to touch the wall. And then I started to retrace my steps, following the smell up the corridor. It faded out: I paced back the other way, but the smell was vanishing, or I was becoming numb to it, and suddenly a door opened and a woman came out, looking at me curiously. I walked past her, turned round abruptly and headed for my room, where I kicked off my boots and got straight into bed. Later I would get out again and run a bath, pouring in purple bubble liquid without stopping until foam towered, in a wobbling, jelly-like mound, above the level of the taps. I lay under it all, listening to the buzzing in my head.

Next morning, there were already children on the train from Carnforth to Arnside, where the walk across Morecambe Bay would begin. A mum, a dad and two boys sat around a carriage table. The littlest boy kept making big, exaggerated yawning noises with his unmasked mouth.

'You're making me yawn!' the dad teased.

'I'm only pretending,' the child said triumphantly.

'Still! It's infectious.'

It was infectious. I cringed in the seat behind them and kept my breathing shallow.

'Stop that. That's enough now,' the mum said.

The dad turned to the boy and smiled. 'I'm not surprised you're excited,' he said.

It was obvious that they were on their way to do the same walk as me. The mum's hair was held back with a pink buff; they all wore shorts and proper walking boots and Osprey rucksacks.

'We should be finished by two. Probably before; it's an eight-mile walk. They just say two because they don't know who's going to be there; some people walk more slowly than others.'

Tiny white birds balanced on the brown sand as it curled and straightened past the train, glistening under the white sky.

'Oh my God, look how muddy it is! And that's just birds! You're going to get muddy feet!' The mum nudged the little boy and laughed.

When the train stopped, I didn't need to look for signs. I got off and followed the family, limply, to the promenade.

'Imagine if we got the wrong dates,' the mum said to the little boy, 'and it turned out to be the nudist walk today!' Awkward, always, to find that the joke you've been sharing with your friends for the past six weeks has been shared by everyone else. It's never a good joke; it's never funny when someone else tells it.

The little boy made blaster gun noises, for no reason except that they were inside him and needed to come out. I winced, the mum winced, and the dad turned round and smiled at him. 'What are you doing? Come here.' He pulled the child closer and ruffled his mouse-blond hair.

At the promenade, the Galloway's Society for the Blind stall was decorated with green and blue balloons. Farther down the beach, they were handing out bright orange T-shirts, with the word MORECAMBE arranged in the vanishing pyramid pattern of an eye test. I avoided the stall. I was already an impostor; I'd never heard of Galloway's Society for the Blind before they let me come along on this walk, and no one was sponsoring me. Children were toddling around in orange shirts as long on them as dresses. I counted two other people of colour: a Black woman laughing with a group of friends, and an East Asian girl leaning her head on a white man's shoulder. Everyone else—perhaps two hundred people—was white, and most of the voices I could hear were middle class. People called out to their friends, took photographs, posed with their Nordic walking sticks. It was a real day out.

EXTREME DANGER, the signs read. BEWARE FAST RISING TIDES, QUICKSANDS, HIDDEN CHANNELS.

Extreme danger. In 2004, under the negligent attentions of a gangmaster, at least twenty-one trafficked people from China drowned in the incoming tide at Morecambe Bay while picking cockles. They had been smuggled into Britain in shipping containers; they were untrained, inexperienced, unsupported, and spoke little English; some were as young as eighteen. When the tide turned on them, one cockler called 999, but could only say 'Sinking water, many many, sinking water . . . Sinking water, sinking water.' He didn't have the knowledge of English to guide the rescuers to where he and the others were struggling. After the tragedy, one Chinese man was convicted of manslaughter and facilitating illegal immigration, and jailed. The two English men who had agreed to pay the pickers £5 per 25kg of cockles were not.

I signed myself in at the welcome stall. The organizer held a sticker out to me and said, with what I considered unnecessary firmness, 'You'll need to display that, please.' I hadn't intended to argue. I put the sticker on my raincoat. It read CROSS BAY WALK on the top, and, underneath, I'M WITH THE POSSE. It was the worst thing I'd ever seen, and I loved it. I sent photographs of myself and the sticker to my friends.

I bought a foul coffee from a machine in a shop that was filled mostly with toys and crystals, and sipped it sitting on the step outside. The bay around the promenade was smooth, almost untouched, with ribbons of silver curving across it. Black-headed seagulls walked importantly in groups, shouting at each other, paddling their feet to bring up the worms. The water lapped the edge of the sand almost imperceptibly, like a horse puckering and lipping food from an offered hand. Everyone clustered conscientiously on the promenade, as though quicksand might be lurking even here in front of the ice-cream shop.

I wanted to use the toilet before we set off. I hated the thought of being caught out in the open, cramping and panicking with people all around me. Balancing my coffee, I started walking back to the public loos, only to stop in dismay; the queue had at least fifty people in it, and registration closed in ten minutes.

I joined the line anyway, listening to people behind me mutter about the pub being closed, or else they'd nip in there and offer them 10p to use the facilities. About how it was fine, surely the organizers wouldn't start the walk without them.

'It's a long walk, you've got to be comfortable while you're doing it!'

'We can catch the others up later.'

'Well, if we get lost, they'll just have to send someone out to rescue us.'

I shuffled angrily, thinking about who expected the world to accommodate them and who didn't; who could be sure of a rescue team sent out to them in this world, and who got swallowed up by it and taken away. The bundle of green and blue balloons by the registration table kicked hard in the wind. I stared out at the sky and felt my vision blur. I hated these people, these British people. Spreading themselves over the world and bending it to their will. And steamrolling everyone else in the process: pushing them deep into the ground without even noticing.

'They say that the water's going to be waist deep at points,' I said conversationally, and aggressively, to the man next to me, without looking at him. 'So if we don't get to use the loo now—it'll be fine. We can just . . . let go, out there. And no one will be any the wiser.'

The man waited to see if I was finished, then laughed with a nervous note in his voice. I kept staring over the railing at the sky.

A marshal came along, eyeing the line anxiously and muttering into her walkie-talkie. The briefing was meant to start at 10.30, and already the minute hand was inching past six. She seemed to come to a decision, and announced that we would get started at any moment. 'The walk must commence at ten forty-five sharp,' she said.

This information had been in the ticket email. 'As Chaucer said: "Time and tide wait for no man"!' The attribution sounded so improbable that I googled it to check, but I didn't have signal.

I fought with myself for a moment, then abruptly left the toilet queue and started walking towards the scatter of orange T-shirts in the distance. I was just the same as everyone else, I thought: angry because I hadn't been able to use the loo before a long walk. It made no sense to get on my high horse.

Underfoot, the dry mud had deep grooves cut through it, dragging it into geological layers, like cliffsides or sheared slate. Suddenly a flicker of white caught my eye. My 'I'm with the posse' sticker had peeled off and was blowing away. I chased it, with that clumsy slow run which tries to be fast enough to catch up, but not so fast that one steps on the blowing-away thing, or makes more wind to blow it away even farther. I caught the sticker—now grimy with sand—and patted it firmly back on my chest. This was not a good sign, I thought. Even inanimate objects were resisting my absorption into the posse. I folded the sticker and my rain jacket together to adhere them even more strongly.

Of course, there was no point in me hurrying. It was ten to eleven by the time the briefing started. Time and tide would apparently wait for these men. Michael—in a yellow fleece—was leading the walk today, he announced through his megaphone. The old guide, Cedric—who was in his eighties—couldn't be there, because his wife had died yesterday. A groan went up from the crowd.

'We're starting out a little late, so you won't make the one-twenty train from Kent's Bank, but there's always the three twenty. It'll be a leisurely walk, it's not a race! If you find yourself in soft sand, don't panic, just move through it quickly! Whistles mean start and stop!'

Everyone cheered, and we started moving: a big ungraceful animal, pulsing forwards.

I was already in a terrible mood. I needed to pee. I was numb, and worried, and already hurting in my shoulders and the small of my back. My bag was very heavy: water, suncream, the books which I'd brought to read on the train but hadn't. I kept letting out one strap of my backpack, then the other, but I couldn't get it evenly balanced. And nothing was flat, from what I could see. Just the raised wall on one side of the concrete track by the beach, with two little Yorkie dogs—inexplicably—trotting along the top of it, and the sand and water down on the other, with children and dogs running in and out. And white people everywhere, in orange T-shirts and buffs. I felt myself floating away.

I overtook two teenage boys and their dad linking arms. They were helping him navigate the tussocky grass. I jumped over a swampy patch, listening to their conversation.

'. . . it's like a PGCE.'

'PGCE or PGDE?'

'They're the same thing. I think. The conditional offer is at Liverpool John Moores; that's where I really want to go . . .'

Grass turned to mud. My boots squelched. The crowd of orange T-shirts carried me forwards; we moved off the path and on to the bay proper. I found myself near Michael, of the yellow fleece, who was talking to a little boy. The little boy hopped over the rocks, and then over a low wall lining our path which was running quickly to a halt. Like all of his kind, he was describing a computer game in extensive and unnecessary detail.

'And what's funny is that there's all these different *llamas*, in all these colours, and they go *pshewpshewpshew!*' He skipped over a damp patch, looking up at Michael.

'Is that right,' said Michael, staring out at the group of several hundred people whose lives he held in his hands. The little boy went on looking up at him.

Suddenly everyone was stopping, taking off their shoes and socks, holding on to each other for balance. I stooped to do the same, wobbling perilously, then moved forwards through the crowd to find out what was going on. It felt so good to be barefoot on that cool wet sand. On my left, a tractor caught my eye, part of the safety measures for our trip; the guide and marshals stood around it, chatting and laughing. Next to the tractor stood an orange-leaved tree, about a foot and a half tall, listing over slightly. There was no other vegetation anywhere. But odder things grow in odder places.

I turned my head away, looked forwards, and then I couldn't look away. There before me was something that looked like heaven. It had crept up on me. Shining flatness, stretching away, into the heart of the light on the horizon. One black-headed gull picked along the edge of the glittering, still water. Horse hooves had imprinted the wet muddy sand. Lots of double shells—I didn't know the name: the ones like butterflies, holding on to each other, nose to nose. Pink and yellow and mauve tracing their delicate insides.

Then, suddenly, I looked up again and out across the water. And I saw it wasn't water but bright land: pockmarked with dunes which held silver light between them. The realization rose up slowly through me, and with it the widest, shining joy. On one side there was a tall hump of greened-over rock; on the other, the distant shore; and, bracketed between them, enough flat land to fill my whole vision and make my skin tingle. Everything was suspended.

I squatted down, digging my heels into the firm, flexible mud, to stare out at it. A dark brown dog darted out in front of me, then dodged behind me again, and I smiled. I stared on, holding the muddy plastic bag with my boots in front of me, for balance. Gradually the noise in my head quietened; the horizon faded and loomed again. I could feel it in my forehead and my ears. With clear air on all sides of my body, I was outlined; I was given shape.

In the distance, near the hump, I could see two square structures, bluish in the haze of the sun that was just starting to come out. But they didn't threaten the flatness. The landscape was in its own scene, in its own time. It was neither past nor future, neither content nor despairing, neither waiting nor fulfilled. The horizon pulled me close.

The tractor chugged on the spot behind me. Big kids—seventeen, eighteen years old—were dashing in and out of puddles, giggling, one girl kicking her heels together. Something had seized them that they couldn't name. I wanted to run straight forwards into that low white light, that flat heaven. What was keeping us?

I stood up, glanced back. Everyone had tied their shoes on to their backpacks; chocolate bars were coming out and being fed into unhurried, chatting mouths, and one small dog was digging in the mud, head down, with an almost vertical fanaticism. Impatient, I turned round again and started walking about in circles, on my own. The mud was like a living skin: it trembled when I put my weight on it, but kept its shape.

And there were softer patches, round and grey, which I thought at first were jellyfish, with sunken circles in the middle. My feet could go straight down into those, at the heel. This was sand making its own physics. Soft in strange places, firm in strange places; holding you away, then sucking you in. When I stepped back, onto the firm mud, a shudder went through it in every direction. The sand was a shape-shifting animal, an alien: something unpredictable, full of history, washed and renewed every day.

A whistle blew. The brown dog ran back to me, and then away. We were moving again. I swallowed my gulp of delight and strode straight toward the flat landscape, throwing myself at its light which gave way endlessly like sliding doors before me.

At first I was in front. But other people walked faster than I could. One person, then another, came between me and that horizon. Some of them were holding hands. As though they needed to hold on to each other, like double seashells, in the face of that improbable landscape. It was easier to walk in the shining tracks left by the tractor; it had rolled the mud into smoothness. Everywhere else it jutted in hard dunes, painful to the bare feet.

A young marshal paused, and stooped to pick up something flat and diamond-shaped. He held it out from his body and took it along with him. A torn piece of map? The rumours carried back through the crowd, towards me.

'A flatfish.'

'Is it a plaice?'

'No, this is a place!' A man gestured comically around, at the flat landscape, and laughed when his wife swiped at him.

It was a place.

I shifted out of the tractor's wake, because sore feet were a small price to pay for clear ground between me and that glowing sky. But more and more people overtook me. Behind me a child was talking to its father.

'. . . so for swimming there are three groups, one for people who need a *lot* of help . . .'

It was a little girl, I knew immediately. That professional, organizing voice starts young. She wanted her father to think her sensible, in a way that a little boy would be too oblivious to think about. Or perhaps wasn't required to be, to be loved.

'. . . one for people who need—just one or two bits of help, and then one for people who're ready to learn new exciting things.'

'And that's in Year Three, is it?' the father said.

'Year Three and just the start of Year Four.'

They'd drawn abreast with me now, father and daughter,

catching me between themselves and the rest of the group. The father wore a big blue rolltop backpack, little glasses perched on his nose, his body a wiry curve against the wind. The child was more blurred, her outline more indeterminate, soft-faced as an infant and tall as a preteen.

'I don't want to step on all these—worms!' she squawked, stooping and hopping. Lugworms had left casts all over the mud, some stained dark blue. The water popped and bubbled where it ran over them, like lips smacking.

'It's not worms! The mud passes through their body and that's what leaves the cast.'

'Still,' said the little girl, not quite understanding, 'I don't want to step on them and hurt them.'

'You won't hurt them! No more than you'd hurt a mole by stepping on a molehill.'

Over to our right there was another tree growing out of the ground: the same height, the same wide leaves, only this time bright green. What were these trees which could withstand the seawater flowing in and out, the salted sand?

The dunes were really hurting my feet. But, I noticed, the pain in my back had gone, and the pressure in my bladder had drawn back. This flat ground was holding me, holding me up. My body was alive again: open to the huge sky. It knew where it was on every side. I couldn't stop and stare, couldn't wander off from the group, but somehow I felt able, just now, to bring that chattering crowd of human presence into focus with the flat place where I lived.

The little girl said something I didn't catch, and the dad responded, 'Yes, that's right. You look down at the ground for a while when you walk, at where you're going right now—and then you look up, into the distance, towards where you want to end up. It's an analogy for life, really.'

A short pause. 'Yes,' said the little girl, in an intelligent voice.

'It's an analogy for life,' the dad repeated. He was pleased with this. 'Like for you, that would be the job you want to do when you're grown up. You do your schoolwork now, but you keep your eye on what you want in the end, and think about how one thing leads to another.'

'Yes,' said the little girl, very decidedly.

A line of seven birds flew horizontally over the shimmering horizon.

This landscape didn't remind me of anything. It was some time before I noticed that. In the fens and in Orford Ness, I'd had flashes of Pakistan: the bare ground and the buffalo wallows. Morecambe Bay was something entirely different. The only ghosts here were the children around me. Children are always ghosts to adults, no matter what they do; they're always shadows of our own fears and memories and rages. No adult can ever see a child properly, through that veil. We've got no idea what they are. We have to just guess, and we can only guess based on what we already know. And we'll always get it wrong.

Still, here there was space to play and experiment: to hop and jump and shift, to try out new things. Every day, on Morecambe Bay, the path had to be renegotiated, made afresh, the safe places moving with the tides and the seasons. No old way through could be relied upon: the guide must watch the bay closely and respond to it. It takes work and love. And we put our trust in him and we made our way through. I looked at the parents in the group—tired and exasperated and human—doing their best to break whatever cycle they found themselves in, on this day out with their family, to find something new and good with the child whom they loved.

It was a dream of a flat landscape. The feeling of unhidden reality without the pressure of memory. Perhaps it was just the luck of the day I'd chosen, with its pearlescent light. Either way, I wanted to put this place on a string and hang it around my neck, to keep.

When we stopped again, it really was at water. A wide stripe of land had taken flight, peeled off from itself: it was moving rapidly from right to left, spreading and banding. We waited for everyone to catch up, and then—as Michael directed—stood in silence for a moment, in memory of the old guide's wife who had died. Everyone was quiet, except for a German Shepherd who cried whenever we stopped. Like me, he was desperate to plunge onwards.

This was the bit I'd heard about, where the water might be waist deep. It needed to be staged with caution. We'd all have to start together into the river. The marshals spread us out along the bank, to make sure there wouldn't be holdups and jams in the middle of the water. Then they set off, wading through the river, leaving us at the water's edge. We watched their yellow T-shirts shrink into the distance. When they were halfway through, and confident that it was safe for us to cross, the whistle blew: we could begin.

The water was cool but not cold; it splashed madly up to my thighs. Lower than I'd been warned, which was good, but no less exhilarating, to be wading fully clothed. The river dragged on me, back and sideways. Its currents joined up with the currents in my body, the pains and tension and pressure always moving through me, and connected them to a bigger network that felt just as real. I was part of something. Not just the river or the landscape. I found myself grinning widely, turning my head to glance at the other walkers. We were all lifting our legs high, in the same inelegant way, failing to coordinate with the water's lapping movement, splashing, walking into it and into ourselves. The smaller dogs hopped along through the water, bouncing to keep their heads afloat like absurd, jaunty puppets.

And suddenly, for the first time, I didn't want to be on the side, by myself. We were all doing this big, strange thing together, and I wanted to be with the others as I did it. I started moving diagonally, trying to wade my way closer to the other people: ridiculous, adorable people, with folding cups hanging off their rucksacks. The tide was strong, and I was still on the outskirts when we made it to the opposite shore, laughing breathlessly. But I'd got a glimpse of something, in the river, even if it hadn't lasted. Even if, on the other side, I was still on my own.

Sandwiches and wraps came out; walkers squatted gingerly on their toes to pour tea from a Thermos into its own tiny cup. All the dogs sat down very neatly and hopefully in front of their owners and gazed up imploringly at their lunches. I was entirely happy. I crouched down, alone, and took a photo of a fish skeleton wrapped around in skin like a cape. Another bone I could note and leave behind. I didn't need to dig it up and bring it with me. I scrabbled through the sand for impossibly tiny snail shells, less than a millimetre long but still recognizable: the whorl, the opening. And every time I looked up, what I needed was still there: the flat bay, ridged and hard, with the thick grey clouds above and a band of brilliant blue just atop the horizon. The flat landscape stayed near me, absorbed in its own inscrutable work, just as I was in mine.

I was happy, crouched there, and I was happy when the whistle blew again and I straightened my legs painfully and we started walking. As noon turned into afternoon, the landscape's light had deepened and intensified. The clouds overhead had grown darker; the bank of light over the horizon had brightened, insistently. Underfoot, the stiff sand ridges were darker, the puddles between them brighter.

It was a landscape growing more and more itself as we walked. If you bent right down to the ground, the ridges looked like tiny mountains. Or, in their clustering multitudes, like gossiping crowds. Like all flatness, if you look close, it's a thousand tiny vibrations.

I found myself again near the father and his little girl. They had pulled ahead of me, and she wasn't talking as much any more. Something was bothering her. As soon as I noticed, so did he, and the quality of his attention changed.

'You'll probably only do this once in your life,' he said. 'And then you'll have done it, you'll have crossed Morecambe Bay! You can tell everybody that. And you'll have the T-shirt to look at and remember what you did.'

'Mmm,' said the little girl. She stopped to fiddle with her big toe, with its dark pink nail polish.

'Are your feet hurting?'

'Yeah.'

'Walk in the tracks.' The dad pointed to the tractor's long silver trail, its double snail-glisten running behind it.

'Why?'

'It's flatter there. It won't hurt your feet as much.'

The little girl moved to her right.

'Better?'

'Yeah.' There was relief in her voice, and the dad relaxed too. It mattered to them both. To go on getting this right.

Birds sauntered around: oystercatchers and black-headed gulls, little speckles of white, not much brighter than the pooled water of the landscape. I'd heard that rarer birds frequented the bay, but today, it seemed, there would be no celebrities. The birds eyed us up as we passed, unsurprised. Smooth ribbons of light crossed the land, wide and penetrating, as though a huge animal had stooped its head and licked a long stripe over the bay.

And suddenly I realized that—at some point—we had made a turn. Flatness was no longer right in front of us, but on our left-hand side: we'd shifted, imperceptibly, towards the green hills and the low white houses nestled beneath them. We were beginning, slowly, to leave the bay. The river crossing had been its climax—how had they engineered a climax, on a flatland walk?—and now we had entered the home stretch. I felt people around me speed up as they realized too. There was something to aim for now, and the air shifted with the refocusing of people's attention. No longer on the wise flat landscape before them, but closing down into tight, refreshing priorities. I heard new phrases enter the conversations around me. People were planning the rest of their afternoons, discussing onward travel. The words 'coffee' and 'cake' came up more than once. And I found myself walking faster, as other people slowed down, bending my way towards the front. I wanted to get to the end now.

We stopped one last time, because the group had thinned behind us into a line of stragglers, and looking back across the bay I could see its line curving right round, like a string of beads: mostly orange, then blue, then a speckling of red and green and black. I was on that string too, another bead. It went all the way back, through 1805, when Wordsworth described his crossing of Morecambe Bay in the *Prelude*, and backwards still further, disappearing into the past.

Waiting for the rest of the posse to catch up, I spotted another of those short, listing trees, and made my way over to it.

I walked around the tree, tugged at it, examined its trunk where it sank into the sand. The angle was strange; it didn't have the thickness at the base which I associated with a rooted tree. Did the tides bring silt up to cover it? I remembered reading about the submerged forests in East Anglia. When the sea levels rose, thousands of years ago, the forests were flooded, and buried gradually in wet silt, the trees preserved perfectly by the anaerobic bog conditions. After the fens were drained, farmers regularly caught their ploughs on black bog oaks in their fields. Could this be the tip of one of those trees poking up? But of course the trees in the bog forests were long dead. Any bony fingertips they poked up out of the earth would be ancient fossils, not springing with green.

A woman came up to me as I studied the tree, smiled doubtfully, as though she was about to speak, then drifted away. A moment later, a man approached, grinning.

'Laurel bushes cost a fortune in the garden centre!'

'Sorry?'

The man repeated himself.

'Oh. Is this laurel, then?'

'I think so. That's what the yellow people were saying.'

'Yellow people' had, I noticed, become the shorthand for the marshals.

'I was asking them about it. They cut the branches fresh every morning, then go out to put them in the sand.'

'Oh!' Realization struck. 'I thought this might be an actual tree. Growing here.'

'No! No, they're waymarkers. To show the safe route. Because it moves, doesn't it? With the wind and the tide, it's always changing. Every morning they find the safe way through and mark it with these branches.'

No green trees, then, in this salt mud; just branches that would slowly turn orange and shrivel, waving the walkers in the right direction. These weren't landmarks you could count on, ones that would stay. Soon they'd stop meaning anything, and you'd have to take your eyes from them and walk on, seeking a new hand to guide you.

The man smiled at me, and I at him. Having nothing more to say, I turned and stared off into the distance. He did too. In angles and short steps, we drifted away from each other, as jerkily as we'd come together.

The tractor rode past, making a beeline for the green grass in the distance. I saw that the little boy from the train was riding on the back, snuggled up to his mum, his eyes half closed.

On the train drawing away from Grange-over-Sands, curling round the bay, I saw the birds we'd been promised: tall white birds like herons, little black ones, birds with curled beaks. I looked them up later, on the RSPB website. Little egrets. Curlew sandpipers. On their light legs they watched the train pull away.

It was too good to talk about, that walk over the bay. I sent photographs of the dead fish to my friends, and told them it was wonderful, and let that suffice. Then I shut my eyes and leaned back in the train seat, alone. And I thought about the waymarkers, the trees which weren't trees at all, stuck into the thick and draining sand. I'd felt such a strong bond with the landscape of Morecambe Bay. I'd felt held by it, connected to it, in sync. And yet I'd read it wrong, totally misinterpreted what I was seeing. The leaves rising up from the flat landscape didn't come from deep roots down inside it. They'd been brought in from elsewhere, driven a few inches in, to flutter for a day or so. What seemed immovable might blow away in a strong enough wind. You could love a thing, it seemed, and not understand it at all.

CHAPTER 5

Newcastle Moor

> . . . specific lives cannot be apprehended as injured or
> lost if they are not first apprehended as living.
> —Judith Butler, *Frames of War: When Is Life Grievable?*

When people outside the northeast of England picture Newcastle, the huge Town Moor might not be the first thing that comes to mind. The green space stretches for a thousand acres, edging some of the most deprived areas of the town, connecting the West End to sleek, studenty Jesmond. If you've got a cow, you can graze it there for cheap, though you'll have to take it in for the winter. But through the summer, anyone can leave their house in a crowded, noisy part of town, and find themselves quickly surrounded by cows.

King John declared the Newcastle Moor common land in 1213, and now it's one of the few urban commons left in Britain. Land for everyone to use. It's bigger, it's often said, than Hampstead Heath and Hyde Park combined, bigger than New York's Central Park. Originally one tract of land, the Town Moor has been carved through by big roads into several small sections: Nuns Moor (north and south), Duke Moor, Hunter Moor, Little Moor, Castle Leazes and, confusingly, a section itself called Town Moor. So much empty land in the middle of a city, doing nothing. What is that moor doing there, when land is at such a premium? Why hasn't it been absorbed, sold, built over?

Since 1774, the moor's been protected by an Act of Parliament, as an area of open space to be maintained in the interests of the city's inhabitants. This means it can't be sold or developed. It's co-managed by the City of Newcastle and the Freemen of the City: an influential medieval institution, with historical rights and responsibilities, whose members protect the moor vigilantly. In 1882, the Freemen allowed a smallpox hospital to be built on it, on the condition that an equivalent piece of land elsewhere was incorporated into the moor. The hospital was demolished in 1958; now it's just a little patch of trees. In the 1940s, a camp to hold Italian prisoners of war was built on the moor, also demolished in the 1950s.

Despite this vigilance, there have been changes in the moor over time. Races were held there in the eighteenth and nineteenth centuries. Most traces of the racetrack were effaced by mining activity in the twentieth century. Coal had been extracted from the moor since at least the medieval period: not for profit back then, since the land was held in common, but used to supply the people of the town with plentiful cheap energy. Mining went on until the late 1940s, alongside everything else. And then the Hoppings— the annual fair held on the moor in the last week of June since the nineteenth century, and now billed as 'Europe's largest funfair'— in turn effaced evidence of the mining, with its fairground rides and stalls and hundreds of thousands of visitors. One thing flattens another, and in the end all that's left is flatness. If you want to see what's happened to the moor, and on it, you have to know what to look for. And even then, you still might not be able to see it.

The moor's plainness is part of the point. It's an active decision. In 1861, the Town Moor Committee proposed developing the moor into a 'People's Park.' There would be 'rides, drives, cricket and drill grounds.' But the Freemen refused. Perhaps they saw the City's efforts as part of a broader creep towards taking control of the land. The moors, they insisted, 'already form the most healthy and extensive public park in the north of England, and perhaps in the kingdom.' And increased development for specialized leisure purposes can be a way of allowing middle- and upper-class uses of the land to trump claims by lower orders. Better, perhaps, to leave it neutral, open, doggedly what it was.

Some of this democratic stance has faded over time. In 1892, a golf course was opened on part of the moor. They built the A167 over another part of it in the 1970s, cutting through the gentle slope of what was once Cow Hill on the southern edge of the moor. They used the spoil to make two small, perky, artificial breasts to replace it. The taller of these mounds has inherited the name of Cow Hill. Viewed from above, they're cupped by a little bra of woodland, tracing round their contours, separating them from the busy main road. But despite these changes, the place still sutures the different sides of the town together. You can step through one graffitied gate in the deprived West End, where rubbish piles up together with fallen leaves by the gateposts—and walk across the moor, whose flat face commits itself nowhere—and step out at the other side, into polished Jesmond, where shining, perfect young people stroll around in fashionable trousers and cropped jumpers. It feels democratic, the moor. Open on all sides. Something like the wood between the worlds in C. S. Lewis's *The Magician's Nephew*: when Polly and Digory put on their magic rings, they're transported to a forest filled with pools of water which are portals to other worlds. The wood, like Newcastle Moor, is a neutral space one passes through, quiet but intensely charged, on the way to transformation. If, indeed, transformation is what one wants.

Our aim will be to keep phase two of the epidemic curve as flat as possible, keeping the number of cases reported each day as low as we can.

At some point in March 2020, when the rumblings from China and Italy had finally become unignorable, a phrase crept into everyone's heads: *flatten the curve*. Cases of coronavirus infection were rising rapidly. Society needed to wash its hands and stay at home, to protect the health services from being overwhelmed by what it became clear was a pandemic. The peaks of infection, hospitalization and death were the enemy. Flatness, unusually, was the word of the zeitgeist.

And it was in the news in other ways too. Stuck in lockdown, everyone was feeling flat. The word proliferated in op-eds, social media posts, advice columns. I became very interested in the way that it stood in for an indescribable emotion. Something which was neither 'scared' nor 'bored,' but a cousin of them. It went without saying, of course, that one wouldn't want to feel flat. People couldn't seem to bear this sensation: of being held in reserve, held back from something. They didn't know how to cope.

Lying on my sofa, or on my rug, I scrolled through the coverage. Everyone, it seemed, was unhappy, except me. On the contrary, I couldn't have been happier. The situation was like a hug, like a weighted blanket. It wrapped around me and held me still. If this was feeling flat, I liked it.

Throughout the spring of 2020, the UK held its breath. Everyone had to be rearranged, spaced out, like a child's carefully arranged toys: no less than two metres apart. If you were really careful, like me, you quarantined and disinfected your post, in case coronavirus came in through your letterbox on the packaging. The government laid down rules: no socializing with anyone outside your household, and you could leave your house just once a day for exercise in the local area. I was living in the West End of Newcastle at the time, five minutes from the edge of Nuns Moor. Before COVID-19 arrived, I'd gone to the adjacent park once a week, to pick up litter in silence near other volunteers, but hadn't really ventured farther. Now that the litter pick had been cancelled, and I'd been assigned a daily walk by government mandate, I suddenly—for the first time—wanted to take one. Unlimited freedom had been too huge and boundless to make any use of: left to my own devices, I mostly just stayed inside. With limits imposed, though, exploration felt newly achievable.

One day in early April, I decided to go on an adventure. I was going to use my daily walk to explore Nuns Moor. I put on my boots—dried mud, left from days or maybe weeks ago, flaking off the laces, in an untidy double knot—and headed out of the door.

At the end of my road, I stepped through a gap in a hedge and into Nuns Moor Park. The verge was studded with stiff green daffodil spikes, just opening out into yellow. Already they'd been enjoyed by children, who'd picked some and crushed some and carried some off. Flowers for all: bread and daffodils for everyone. I made my way through the park, to the little green gate in the corner, shaded by wet leaves. I'd seen it before, but it hadn't ever occurred to me to go through it. I was still too used to eliminating possibilities before I'd entertained them, filing them preemptively under 'for other people—not for me,' because that's how things had been in Pakistan. Time to make the jump. A sign on the gate warned: CATTLE OPENLY GRAZE THIS AREA FROM MARCH TO NOVEMBER. A note, I thought, of incredulous, well-heeled outrage in the tone there. Openly grazing, undeterred by scandal or police presence.

I closed the gate behind me with a clang, and South Nuns Moor stretched wide, like mint in my throat. A huge empty green space, patched with yellow, bordered by trees. Turning and scanning the flatness was like having one's head and neck nape stroked, slowly. Everything was still, except the one or two dog walkers making their way unhurriedly across the moor, a little flutter of the taller yellow grasses and, at the far end, the to and fro of cars beneath and beyond the trees. Something about the way they flashed between the trunks slowed them down, silenced them, till they looked and felt like beetles scurrying. It took a moment or two to spot the cows. Like stars: once you'd caught sight of one, the rest came into view.

Paths cut through the moor in every direction. Between, there were hard, small hummocks to step up onto and almost fall off, cowpats sunken and drying into cracks. It was disorganized land. Unarranged into anything. Not a park, not a field, not a farm. And yet it took time to look across it. It took time to walk across it. It felt like duration made into space.

And this was only Nuns Moor. If you kept going, the moor did too. I'd lived in Newcastle for a year already; the moor started minutes from my front door, and there was so much of it, lying unexplored. That was fine with me. Nuns Moor would do me for now, and perhaps always. I liked going to the same places, again and again.

I walked round the edge of the moor, and then diagonally back across the middle, returning to my starting point. Night was beginning to fall. Starlings gathered there, clustering in the trees and shrieking to each other, breaking free of the land as I approached and scattering themselves across the sky. That rhythm of moving and bursting felt like a compact between me and the birds and the sky. It felt like a sign that the landscape was coming into itself: flinging itself upwards, into shapes without meaning.

Lockdown meant that, finally, I had a reason not to see anyone. Keeping in touch with my friends sometimes felt like painting the Forth Bridge. As soon as I'd seen them all, had coffees with them all, dinner, an outing, a walk, it was time to start again. Now no one was allowed to see anyone. I could sit on the floor, lost in reverie. I could gaze fixedly at the objects around me: the cat's scratching post, the table, the stones arranged by the fireplace. When I phased out, and returned some time later, they would still be there, unchanged. And I could focus on the constant thrum of reactions, just below the waterline of my mind. Anything I tried to distract myself with only added to the noise; now I could finally sort through it, by myself.

The last time I'd visited my mother, in Scotland, I'd recklessly taken away with me a small pile of photographs of our time in Pakistan. I'd told myself that I needed these photographs more than anyone else. I would actually look at them, rather than hoarding them unseen in a cupboard. Like all our communally owned things, though, there were strict, cultish rules about them: how they were to be used, looked at, discussed, stored. So I just stole them and said nothing.

I did look at them. I looked and looked at them. I spread them out on my floor. Before lockdown, I'd shown them to my therapist, to my best friend, to the girl I loved. I held them out, over and over again, as totems of the way I felt. Everyone who loved me looked at the photos and tried to find a way to respond. But they meant nothing to anyone but me.

I'd chosen the photographs to torture myself. All the ones which made me uncomfortable, which contradicted my own memories and feelings. There was one of me sitting on my father's lap, looking unsmiling up at the camera as he held half a guava to my mouth. One of me standing next to my father, with one hand on his leg as he held Forget-Me-Not. The other rested, dramatically, on my stomach. As though I was about to declaim something. Or as though I was in pain.

The one that I looked at longest was him—skinny as a pole, wearing a jumper that Rabbit would later adopt as a teenager—with his hair not yet entirely grey, throwing me into the air. I was such a tiny baby, in that photo, that my body didn't hinge in the middle. I soared above his head as a single, solid unit: a little bundle of baby.

All of these photos showed a side of my father that I had no memory of. I remembered, once, being carried on his shoulders, and being incredulous, even in the memory, about what was happening. Holding my legs really still, in his hands, so that he wouldn't get annoyed and put me down. Everything else I remembered was a blur, or an act of violence. A remote control being thrown at me. A slap.

But those were just my memories. This was proof of something different. A good father. A caring father. If it came to a trial, say—if there were such a thing as a trial—then we had proof of his side and not of mine. His students would step up to say what a good man he was. His mother and father, his sister and brother, would all testify to his character. And on the witness stand for the opposition, there would be only me, shaking and tongue-tied. *I know what I know*, I would whisper. And of course that would never be enough. I would never be able to explain.

I sat for hours, quietly shuffling through my thoughts, again and again. Like a pack of cards; like my sheaf of photographs. I took them out, pulled off the rubber band, combed through what I already knew by heart.

And yet, somehow, in between all my rumination, or maybe because of it, I was achingly happy. Now I had space and time to think all the way to the end of a thought without having to interrupt myself and put on a face for another person. Daily life had always felt like the Magic Slate we'd played with when we were little. You start drawing, hoping to get somewhere, but then—when you're nearly finished— a flash of distraction or fear or intervention pulls the side of the slate out and clears it completely. But in this locked-down world, language was slowly rising up towards me, taking shape around my memories and feelings, and the flat place inside me.

And it was even more than that. The catastrophe had come for me once again, and for the first time in a long time I felt real, because I knew how to cope with catastrophe. I'd done it before. I'd grown up in confinement; its rhythms were braided into me. And where those rhythms made me move awkwardly through a world where I was expected to desire, aspire, explore, adventure—against all the lessons of my early life—now, for the first time in years, I was moving along the grain instead of against it. Incredibly, I was *adapted* for the situation I found myself in. Growing up behind chicken wire in a house of crisis meant I knew how to deal with the worst happening. This was the worst, or a version of it. All my muscles relaxed. The new normal was my normal.

This is how you do it. You make very small plans, the size of five or ten minutes, and you make them one at a time. You eat away at things, like tackling a bowl of porridge with a teaspoon. You're allowed to have the teaspoon, to be slow and impractical, because there's a pandemic. You don't look behind you or in front, because there's nothing you can do about anything but the present. You don't miss other people, because ultimately you feel safest in your own company.

In a sense, complex PTSD is a condition which only gains meaning beyond the situation that caused it. You adapt to the world you find yourself in. Your mind and body learn what they need to do to function, as well as they can, in that world. So if you grow up in a confined, unpredictable, frightening environment, you learn not to crave novelty, because if there's any on offer, it's probably dangerous; you learn to go numb when bad things happen, because you have no choice but to wait them out; you learn that plans and dreams and expectations can be shattered in a second, so it's better to give up having them; you learn to trust no one but yourself. That's sensible. Logical. If you stay in that environment, those instincts can help to keep you alive. It's when you *leave* that environment that they become maladaptive. Then—only then—are you a damaged person. You have to laboriously unlearn all those habits, and invent new ones, in a world whose very calmness feels frightening and unreliable to you.

Except now the tables were turned right round again. I found myself back in a world I was easily, keenly adapted to. I was flying.

I got more done in those first few weeks of lockdown than I'd managed in the whole previous year. I drafted great chunks of academic work. I made bad art, every day. I made puppets. I slept as much as I wanted to, which was a lot. I knew my happiness was indecent, and that it would grate on people who, quite reasonably, expected their lives to be broadly safe and predictable—who hadn't been primed to a lifetime of fearful tedium. I couldn't have been luckier, really. I worked from home, I was an introvert, and I was intimately familiar with pain and horror already. Everything was fine, and I knew how to get myself through this landscape. I knew what every step felt like.

My mother was cheery, too, when we spoke or messaged. She'd been one of the first, annoyingly, to foresee the pandemic, making doomy noises about it since January. I hadn't taken them seriously: during the swine flu pandemic of 2009, when I was twenty, she'd come into my room where I was unpacking from a term at university, and gravely advised me to make a will, because a third of the world's population was likely to die. 'Who knows?' she said. 'It could be any one of us.' My mother was always alert to catastrophe, always ready for it, bringing her braced, practical face. It was annoying that on this one occasion, like a stopped clock, she was right.

Luckily it wasn't in her nature to make a big deal out of her victory. She got on with things, as usual; she swiftly formed a bubble with an acquaintance, and they went on walks together with the neighbour's little fluffy dog, my mother soberly checking her step count every so often to make sure she got her ten thousand.

My walks are great, she messaged me, *my bean plant is growing ever taller!*

When my mother folded herself up and packed herself cosily into catastrophe, it infuriated me. But of course, she and I were just the same, in this.

Here's a pic of the spider plant baby you gave me, I messaged back. *Look how big it is now.* The spider plant dangled a trail of its own new babies over the side of the bookshelf.

The daffodils went back into the ground, and it was summer. I came back to the moor, every day, crisscrossing over the same space in different directions. I even took up running for a while, jogging around the moor's tarmac paths and mud paths and desire lines: the paths marked out by footfall alone, as people found their own ways through. The moor's a popular place to run. People in purple lycra or baggy tracksuits are always panting up and down its paths, sometimes pushing buggies as they go. A jolty ride for the babies, but maybe they like it.

So I ran, too, imagining myself getting stronger, waiting for the surge of energy that I'd heard exercise would bring. But one day my vision went strange in the middle of my run: coloured chevrons and black and white tiles started streaming past my eyes, and I stumbled home, yawning great cracking yawns and picturing myself falling asleep right there in the road. That was the end of my running. I decided to wait till I had some blood pressure to speak of. Until then, I would walk.

If I saw people I knew on the moor, from my neighbourhood or the local litter pick, I stayed relaxed. Gathering was not permitted. It was actually, blessedly, illegal to go over and talk, or—worse—to submit myself to being hugged, in a bloodless automatic performance of affection from people I barely knew. They were only allowed to wave at me from a distance and shout, 'HELLO! HOW ARE YOU! EVERYTHING'S SO WEIRD, ISN'T IT! SEE YOU SOON!' And then go on. No stopping to chat! Dangerous!

And if I felt lonely at this time—which was hardly ever— there were always the cows, openly grazing, in their brazen way, on the moor. Most of the grazing cows are being fattened for meat, nowadays. They are sturdy and beautiful, with little toupees atop their heads and yellow tags in their ears: russet, dark brown, black and white. They look at you as you pass, sometimes sternly, but if you haven't got a dog, they don't give you trouble. If you have got a dog, and the dog pisses them off somehow, then they approach very slowly and glare. They never minded a whippet I sometimes walked for a neighbour, who would stop on the edge of the moor and stare tragically at me (the dog, not the neighbour, of course).

The cows were sometimes on one side of South Nuns Moor, sometimes on the other. People say that cows lie down when rain is coming. But the moor cows lay down, and stood up, and I found out that neither meant anything, in terms of the weather. Once I found three of them arranged in a kind of triskelion shape, tail to tail and gazing implacably out across the moor. 'Hello, gorgeous!' I catcalled as I passed, and they said nothing.

If I found a lost glove on the moor, or a strange flower, that was a big event. I would squat right down, swaying, wet grass brushing against my knee and my bum, and study the thing. I would look fully until there was nothing left to see—for minutes at a time—and then I would walk on.

If I shut my eyes as I walked, the most that would happen was that I might step in a cowpat, or bump my boot against a hummock. I could phase out for as long as I needed—spring right out of my body, with a lurch, and heave up into the weightless sky, or sink into the dark film beneath my eyes till they watered with being left open, unblinked. And when I slid back into my vision, everything was still as I had left it. No one was stooping over me asking if I was all right. I hadn't wandered into traffic. Nothing had broken.

And I couldn't get lost on South Nuns Moor. I could see the whole huge space all at once. I could walk there until I was tired, and my knees felt weak, and I would still be right there. If it was a nice day, I could lie down in the pale hot grass and look up at the sky, next to dark brown cowpats: almost square, with yellow flies walking over them looking like fruit studded in dark loaf cakes. If rain was rolling in, I could keep going around the perimeter, until I found the blue gate at the top of the park, or the green gate at the bottom end, and make my way through the park and home, to sleep.

'You grew up in Pakistan? Wow—I wouldn't have guessed. You sound—yeah! So English. You could be on the BBC. So what was Pakistan like?'

When I was younger, I used to say it was terrible. But then I'd see the speaker misunderstanding—their minds drifting to terrorism and burqas—and I'd hurry to clarify. In my family, I explained, we stayed inside and spoke to no one and did nothing, and were wholly controlled by my father. That was what was awful. Not Pakistan itself. I had no idea, really, what a normal life in Pakistan was like. I couldn't speak for it.

The British person would look blank and disappointed. 'But . . . isn't that quite normal, in Pakistan?'

And I'd feel embarrassed. As though I was complaining about nothing. A normal thing, which happened to everyone Over There: hardly worth remarking upon. It wasn't normal, of course; most families in Pakistan visit cousins and friends, spend time at weddings—all the things my father refused to waste his time on. But as far as British people seem to be concerned, all women in Pakistan stayed behind curtains, or veils, or walls, and that was just the way it was. So why complain about it? Worse things happen in places like that. Presumably.

It wasn't until the pandemic that I realized this was a racist double standard. When coronavirus slammed the world up against a wall, I began to feel, keenly, my damage. Because everyone around me was complaining—with a desperate, demanding, aggressive edge to their voices—about the lockdown. It was inhumane to keep us inside, they said. Inhumane to have no human contact, no touch. While I was breathing easier for the first time in years, everyone around me was going mad: scratching themselves out of their skins and howling. Worst of all, children in the UK were kept from their friends, from sports and socializing and after-school activities. What would happen to these children? Would they be stunted, broken, permanently damaged by this year of isolation?

I had to bite my mouth to stop myself from being unkind. Because I knew which children mattered and which didn't. What children in other countries were expected to endure as standard parts of life—cramped conditions, imprisonment, periods of separation from loved ones—must not be tolerated for British children; unlike their counterparts abroad, they are fragile, precious, capable of infinite sophisticated development.

And I felt vindicated. Because what I'd endured for sixteen years—what British people had told me was trivial, didn't sound that bad, might be something just to hurry up and get over, like all the other inconvenient accoutrements of being brown and from the Global South—was now sending those same people into hysterics.

That was the point at which I understood, deeply, that I really was different from other people. Generally, I had assumed that life was hard for everyone, and perhaps I was more intolerant of its stresses than most. But now I realized that human contact really did make other people feel better. It wasn't like a beam of blistering heat, only tolerable for short stretches. Something in the world's everyday organization was fundamentally soothing to them: the going to work, being at work, talking to other people. And when that comfortable, liveable world was taken away, they fell apart.

In 2003, I learned, there had been a competition to find 'Britain's worst wasted spaces.' And an architecture student had nominated Newcastle's Town Moor. 'The moor is one of the largest urban open spaces in Britain,' he argued, 'yet its potential is currently wasted.' It was interesting, I thought, as I lay on my living-room floor, wasting my time in the way I liked best, that the moor had once been so intensely used—for races and mining and hospitals—and was now used so minimally, in capitalist terms. And of course that got counted as waste, in the same way that we didn't know how to assign a value to doing nothing or going nowhere. We don't know how to look at places which don't *do* anything.

I practised looking at the moor. I looked at it on my walks, in motion, and when I lay down on the ground I looked at it from grass level, and one day I opened Google Maps to look at it from above. On the screen, I could see strange markings, particularly on the east side of the Town Moor section, faint yellowish lines worn into the dark green grass, and to the west, a white cross and three little white dots. Unexplained. Could it be the foundations of a chapel? Or another archaeological remnant?

After digging around online and finding nothing, I emailed the City Council's Archaeology department, and begged for the most recent archaeological report, from 1995. It turned out that the lines were the last traces of the eighteenth-century racecourse. But what was the cross, and what were the white dots? The cross was especially mysterious: it seemed to be connected to a small square, off to the side, by a little line. What was that square? A well for my hypothetical chapel? The survey didn't help me here: I didn't have the aerial photos I needed to cross-reference with the codes, and its descriptions of locations made my directionally stunted brain creak and freeze. I went back to Google, trying to puzzle it out, without success.

The artificial hills in the southwest of Town Moor were causing me further difficulty. Colloquially, they get called Cow Hill and Race Hill. But the real Cow Hill, of course, is long since lost, and the survey seemed to suggest that the real Race Hill coincided, somehow, with the racecourse; way off to the east of where the artificial one now stood. Phantom hills, appearing and disappearing, shifting around on the moor like a mouse under a blanket. One turned into another; they died and were resurrected. I switched on the Google Maps terrain indicator, but all the hills on the moor were too low to register. From above, flatness.

As I worked my way through the archaeological survey, there was a section about Exhibition Park—a small area of the moor developed into a traditional park, like Nuns Moor Park—which stunned me. Exhibition Park was named after the North East Coast Exhibition of Industry, Science and Art, held there in 1929. Among the exhibits was an 'African village'—a human zoo inhabited by a hundred Senegalese people, less than a hundred years ago.

This isn't ancient history. My grandmother would have been seven. Within living memory, like so much of the racism the West sweeps under the rug, claiming it was acceptable at the time.

It was never acceptable at the time. In fact, I discovered, an MP protested against the 'African village' in Parliament.

> Does the hon. Member . . . not realise that, though [the human zoo] may not be repugnant to the exhibition authorities here, or to the British visitors, it is very repugnant to the educated section of Africans, and does he not further realise that we are only making an exhibition of the wretched way in which citizens are reared up and kept in the British Empire?

The protestor was Shapurji Dorabji Saklatvala, who was MP for Battersea North for much of the 1920s. An MP of Indian Parsi descent. In 1929. Certainly not what racist Brits imagine when they think of the 1920s.

Two things rose to the top of my mind as I researched the human zoo in Newcastle. First: People of colour have always been here, in Britain's flat places, living and struggling. Violence and oppression form the bedrock of the landscape that I recognize and move through.

Second: People have always been protesting. It's just that no one has been listening.

By midsummer, most lockdown restrictions had been lifted. Instead, it became legally required to wear a mask in enclosed public spaces, like shops and buses. Restaurants could open again, and social restrictions were relaxed. I started seeing my friends, a little, and enjoyed it. Since we were still only really meant to meet outside, we went on walks to all the beautiful parts of the North East, and I fell deeper and deeper in love with that part of the UK. People flocked outside to enjoy the moor. And with people came police, strolling around on Nuns Moor like they owned the place. My area was noisy, messy, multicultural, over-policed, under-resourced. Full of things happening openly, like hunger and deprivation and violence. None of this was the police's concern, not when they could go into restaurants and shout at the (brown) owners to raise their masks, or swoop down on two Black boys loitering by the tennis court. The officers went round in pairs, and smiled at me. I glowered back.

I was angry. Not just with the police: with everyone. White people seemed to be rushing back to their old freedoms with a huffy air of entitlement. They expected the world to fit around their needs, and were furious when it stopped doing so. I understood people being distressed about the actual pandemic, the fear of infection and death, or the loss of their loved ones. I also felt viscerally upset for people worried about losing their jobs or living in poverty. Those made perfect sense to me as complaints. What made me boil, though, was the hysteria about things not being 'normal': people panicking and outraged when the world just stopped moving to the social rhythms they preferred. I had had to adapt to a world that certainly didn't match mine—that often felt unliveable to me—and when I didn't, I was called stubborn or spoilt. But when white people had been asked to adapt to a world which was even temporarily different from that which they were used to—where they stayed at home, or wore masks in shops, to protect the elderly and the vulnerable—they'd sat down and screamed like toddlers in a supermarket.

And then I felt contemptuous, at how weak British people seemed to be. How thoroughly they had internalized the idea that the world would always fit fluidly around them and their needs. Why, I kept thinking, was what I had gone through in Pakistan acceptable, if lockdown was a crime against our humanity? I'd lived a life so isolated that after sixteen years in Pakistan I still was not fluent in Urdu. Thousands and thousands of people lived lives like that, all over the world. Not just certain groups of women in Pakistan and Afghanistan and Saudi Arabia. Not just families in China, where children didn't see their parents for months, because they worked far away to send money home. Even in Britain: immigrants living eight to a bedroom in slum housing. Disabled people, forced to spend their lives indoors because councils stopped funding their personal assistants. Refugees trapped in detention centres. Were those lives defunct, not worth living well? Was my life worthless? Or was it just accepted that some lives could, and would, and *should* expect to hold more pain than others?

And I started to feel more stubborn about my own life, and what I wanted it to look like. If white people could rend their hair and wail about not being able to go to the pub, I too had a right to experience certain conditions as intolerable. Liking people was no more logical and natural than not liking people. I would never again accept whole days in proximity to others. I would never again force myself into unbearable relationships.

———

'Oh God. And you're all alone! I wish I could be there with you!'

As usual, my friends were worried about me. Many of them had fled back to their families in March, before the first lockdown began, to wait it out in company. But it was different in my family. We'd held a single group call to decide what to do. In the end, Spot had gone back to Scotland in case my mum got ill and needed help, and the rest of us stayed put, where we had jobs to get on with.

Ours was not the kind of family where questions of comfort and companionship took precedence over practical concerns. That was more than fine with me. I was most comfortable and companioned here, on my own, anyway. But my friends didn't see it that way.

'It really is fine,' I insisted, smiling at the screen even though we were on a voice call. 'I feel great. Literally, I'm the best prepared anyone could be for this. Staying inside all the time and not seeing anyone. I've been preparing for this my whole life.'

As we spoke, I was crouching on the floor next to the laptop, cradling a hot-water bottle against my stomach. It was starting to get colder, as summer slipped now into autumn. And I'd discovered that when I felt most dissolved in the middle of my body, heat helped a bit; it brought my stomach back into one piece and reassured me that it was staying put. Since I was at home all the time, I could carry a hot-water bottle around with me from room to room. In fact, who would stop me, I thought, if I kept on hugging it in public after all this was over? Why not? Who cared?

'I just don't think it can be good for you.' My best friend sounded stressed. 'I know it feels good right now, and maybe it's good for you to have a break from people? For a bit? But in the long-term you do need to see people or you'll go mad.'

It was hard to explain to my friends that this was absolutely the opposite of what was happening. More and more, I was realizing, in my ordinary British life—before the pandemic, anyway—it was possible to pin down the specific times when the flat place took me back, unannounced, unconsenting. It was when people were looking at me. My throat would close. I found myself with nothing to say. A noise in my head like a starling leaping up, piping pointlessly, falling back down to the earth. The flat landscape I walked through in my mind, alone, at those times—myself the highest point in all that waste—glittered and shone. I knew that its febrile shine was because it was drenched. I was drenched. But not with fennish floodwaters, or a roaring inland sea. This is the sparkle of cortisol, the saline gleam of adrenaline. Living with complex post-traumatic stress disorder means living in a sea of stress hormones, all the time. I wake up into dread. Someone's casual movement, glimpsed in my peripheral vision, sends me spiking. So in a room of people, all moving and fidgeting all the time, meaninglessly, I can barely see through the panic.

Lockdown had been very good for that, so far. It turned people into contained squares on a laptop screen. And when I needed to, I could turn off my camera and lie down, until my body coincided with itself again. This got faster and faster. I was eating more, putting on weight, breathing more deeply. The more my body got used to feeling safe, and knowing that it could have what it needed to feel safe, the stronger I felt. More able to endure the parts of the world which might always hurt, because the quiet of lockdown gave me proof that they wouldn't last forever.

'Honestly. I feel amazing.' We had had so many versions of this conversation already. 'Listen, it's other people who stress me out and make me feel mad. And now I have an amazing excuse not to see them. I don't have to go anywhere or see anyone, and I can just think and work and cuddle the cat.'

'I'm so glad you have her.' The thought of the cat seemed to comfort my best friend.

I was glad, too.

I'd got the cat the previous October. After longing for a cat for years and years and years—since I was a child, and having a cat was yet another entry on that list of simple but impossible things—I was still hesitant. I didn't have a permanent job yet, and I might have to move house, maybe even somewhere the landlord wouldn't allow cats. Or overseas, which would be terrifying, for me and for the animal. I'd met a cat once who'd moved to London from France. His name, unfortunately, was Pierre. 'He has never been the same since,' his owner had explained to me. Pierre sat crouched on the table, like an obese grey toad between us, with a veteran's thousand-yard stare. 'He used to be very lively. But he only speaks French, you see. So London is very cold to him.'

With poor, traumatized Pierre on my mind, I put off getting the cat, thinking I should wait until I was stable and secure. Until one day, quite suddenly, I couldn't stand not having one any longer, perhaps in the way that—I'm told—many women are seized imperiously, in their thirties, with the need to have a baby. Abruptly I wanted a cat more than I was deterred by the reasons not to get one, and I went out to all the cat shelters in Newcastle. Morvern was in the last centre I looked in: a stroppy little black queen, three years old, who either hid in the cat tree or strolled around methodically hissing at all the other cats. Her eyes were green, like a witch's familiar, and the next day I arrived with a cat carrier and took her home.

Morvern slept under the bed, and in my jumper drawer, and on top of the bookshelf, and on the windowsill, and most of all on my legs whenever I held them still. She chirped whenever she came into the room, whenever I woke her up by pushing my face into her dark body, whenever I called her name. When I sat on the floor with my laptop, she twined round me; when I turned to her, she turned her inscrutable, lizard-like face up to mine and sniffed my cheeks. Her breath smelled of turkey biscuits and spit.

Cats do not understand smiles. So Morvern didn't care whether I smiled or not. What mattered to Morvern was my presence and my hands and my voice. My face could stay dull and expressionless, unless she broke a real tender smile out of me by putting both paws on my leg and leaning up to see what I was doing. That was a gift which gave itself to her, effortlessly. If I was feeling especially numb and distant, words choked up in my throat or my head caught in the tide, all I needed to do was chirrup back to her chirrup, with a kind of brief hum in my throat. During lockdown we talked like this for hours, chirping back and forth.

I wasn't stable or secure. But Morvern jumped over the shifting tectonic plates of me, walking carefully around my dirty coffee mugs, settling on my book piles. The night she arrived, she burrowed down under my covers to sleep in my arms, and I realized then that nothing could be allowed to get too bad any longer, because if I died, who would feed Morvern? When I wanted to die—which still happened now and then, even during lockdown, like a habitual safe place that my brain went to when it was tired—the fantasy halted as soon as I reached Morvern. Morvern might not like a new home; they might not know how she liked to play—with trailing things, like ribbons, not balls, dragged slowly over the floor. (I only found this out by accident; the people at the cat home had told me she wasn't interested in playing. But one day I was winding up a tape measure, letting it trail on the floor, and she pounced.) And a new owner might not know that if you walked straight towards her, she got scared and ran away. You had to give her time and space: to move slowly around her. Another home might try to make her befriend other cats. So that wouldn't work. I scowled at the warm dark bundle of her, a speed bump on the road to my death, and after a while I moved on to thinking about other things.

Mostly what Morvern did was to come and find me, wherever I was sitting in the flat, and to curl her tail around her feet and hunch into a ball, near me but facing away. I did some research. This meant, the internet said, that she was keeping watch for predators for both of us. This meant that she loved me.

I loved her too. Unsmilingly, facing away, drifting in neutral. I loved her so much.

On a crisp, bright day that autumn, when all the hawthorns and rowans in Newcastle were showing their red berries against a deep blue sky, I went a little farther on the moor. I climbed over the fence around South Nuns Moor, carefully crossed the road, and climbed into Hunters Moor. This one was a bit less flat, the land rising up and down with trees scattered, but still blank enough for me to drift over without thought. On either side a block of student accommodations, or maybe a block of council flats, I wasn't sure, rose into the sky. At the corner I climbed over the fence, again, to inch over the busy A167 that wound itself into a multi-stringed knot at the centre of four moors, and paused on the bridge to look down at the cars which shot beneath. On the other side there was a sign which matched the 'Cattle Graze Openly Here' one from Nuns Moor, backed up by a thicket of trees. I ducked in and found myself suddenly plunged into a dark, slippery woodland. Pulling myself up the muddy track, trying not to slip—in my too-worn black boots which had started letting in water, but which I liked too much to stop wearing—past the strange pieces of rubbish (signs, broken tents) which someone had left there, I burst at the top of the slope into light barred by a pointy-topped fence. Someone had folded the fence into a split: a gap I could edge through if I took my backpack off. And then I was at the top of the hill: the taller one, which stole its name from Cow Hill.

I didn't like going down the hill. It was easy to slip. I walk strangely on hills, I'm told: gingerly, each toe pointing downwards as I step. It's not a tall hill, but it took longer to descend than I expected, and I was tired by the time I was halfway down.

Nevertheless I urged myself further out still. Past the hills, away towards the mysterious east of Town Moor, where the old racing track raked the ground in a loop. I'd determined to get to the bottom of those white dots and that cross, which I could see from above on the terrain view of Google Maps. It was a good day: the sun was out, shining warm into my hair even though the air was crisp as an ice chip, and I took off first my jacket then my hoodie. The white dots, when I reached them, were square concrete areas which had obviously at some point involved plumbing; there were pipe-shaped holes going into the ground, and a copper-stained drain cover, and other holes concreted in, just drawn circles. On one of the squares, a clump of plants shot thickly and drastically out of the pipe holes by the drain cover, towering anarchically high above the neatly cropped grass that surrounded the area. Perhaps these had been cow troughs? I paced over them for a while, then turned and made towards the cross, following the blue dot which traced my passage on my phone screen.

As I approached, I could see that the cross wasn't concrete. Just flattened grass. And over to one side of it, a man in a grey woolly beanie and big green jacket was fiddling with a piece of machinery, standing next to a little folding stool. An archaeologist, I thought, my heart quickening. Investigating the site! But as I approached further, I could see he was holding a remote control.

'Flying something?' I called. He looked at me and said nothing. I approached and stood a little way off from him, gazing into the sky. It was a radio plane, I saw now. We watched it sail around the blue, streaked with contrails from real planes.

After a while, the man said to me: 'Just like flying a kite!'

'It looks like it! And it doesn't make much noise, either!'

'Remember flying a kite when you were little?' the man continued, as if I hadn't spoken. 'Relaxing. Therapeutic.'

Kite-flying in Pakistan was neither relaxing nor therapeutic. In springtime, Punjab celebrated the festival of Basant. It was originally a Hindu festival, which caused some unease in Pakistan. But on either side of the national border that bisected the province, for those few days in spring, people celebrated by dressing in yellow and orange, and flying paper kites. These were squat and square, with a little skirt and coloured shapes stuck on for decoration— and beneath the kite itself, a string coated with ground glass and metal filings, sharp to the touch. Flying kites in Lahore was all about fighting: the point was for one kite to sever the strings of others in mid air. All over the city, paper kites which had lost the battle fluttered down to the flat roofs and the roads, to be swept up by gleeful children. Abandoned strings were a major hazard: they could short-circuit the exposed power lines, or even—pulled taut across a road—slit someone's throat as they cycled along. So Basant, and all kinds of kites, have been banned intermittently since the noughties, fuelling an underground trade and illicit nighttime flying sessions.

We weren't allowed to fly kites. Once—and I remember this vividly—we were allowed out on the roof to watch other children flying them. I gathered up the kites that fell down to us, and thrilled.

On the moor, the man and I stood for a while together, in silence. The motor switched on and the plane began to drone, a little.

'If you're feeling adventurous, you can do little tricks,' the man said.

'Ah! Loop the loop!'

And the plane did indeed loop the loop.

'Thank you for showing me!' I said, as loudly as I dared, and the man grinned, eyes still on his remote. 'I don't suppose you know what this area is, do you? This kind of cross shape?' I gestured around.

'We used to mow it in a square,' the man said. 'But now we just do a cross shape. It takes less time. And with the wind coming either from north or west, it's the right direction for the planes to go, anyway. Runways, you see.'

'You make this cross? To fly planes?'

'As I say,' the man said, 'we used to do it in a square. But a cross is quicker. You can see, down there,' he motioned with his head, 'the area over there, where you get the planes started up. And then you bring them along the path to the runway, here. And you go either that way,' he gestured along one arm of the cross, 'or that.'

'Ah!' I was laughing now. 'I thought—I had it in my head it was an archaeological site! Like a church, or something! I could see it on the map!'

I half made to show my phone to him, then thought better of it. The man was already shaking his head. 'You'll have to speak up. I can't take my eye off the plane! When you get to my age, you can't do two things at once. Brain and eye and hand, got to keep them all in line.'

I went down the path to look at the mown square, where the model planes got started up, and then walked back to the runway where the man was now flying the plane low in the sky.

'I'm so glad I met you,' I shouted. 'If I hadn't, I'd never have known this place was for flying planes! I had all these other ideas in my mind!'

The man landed the plane, looked at me, and grinned. The plane was, I could see, made of white polystyrene, grubby on its underside, its wingspan about the length of his arm. 'Are you at the university? You can go and tell them all: Call off the troops! It's a false goose chase over here.'

A false goose chase. I liked that. I put my hoodie back on and headed home.

I'd got the land wrong, again. I'd misread it. But I wasn't upset. It was exhilarating that something could spread itself out so clearly to me—impress itself so indelibly on my mind and my heart—and then, with a few words from a stranger, be transformed. The people I met in flat landscapes knew things that I didn't. They could identify plants, find paths through quicksand, fly planes; they saw and used the landscape in a very different way from me. And the more of them I met, the less alienating I found this.

I've only been to the golf course on the moor once, when it was buried under snow. As winter returned in late 2020, and infection rates surged once again, the UK was sent into its second national lockdown. You were allowed to meet up with one other person in an outside public space. So I met a friend in Kenton, on a freezing cold day, and we staggered around on our walk in the icy wind. Unable to find shelter, which would break the coronavirus rules, we had to keep moving. Our boots sank into the snow: deep on the level ground, lurchingly deep when we let it take our weight directly above a bunker. Golf is a treacherous waste. Like money, it digs holes in the world. When I got home, worn out from having seen another person—struggling through the bunkers, flinging words over my shoulder, overwhelmed—I flopped down and slept, in a cowl of heat.

Snow kept coming that winter. The golf course stood empty: land designed for the use of an exclusive few, overspecialized, useless in the face of extreme weather. In contrast, the rest of the moor knew what to do with itself. In February 2021, another icy Beast from the East storm hit the UK, and everyone ran out to Cow Hill with their sledges, whether or not it was permitted. With every screaming, giggling chute down the hill, the snow compacted more and more tightly into slippery ice.

I didn't go, of course. But it was nice to see photographs of the sledgers, on social media, and to know that everyone was having fun. Even people without sledges came, people without money for sledges: they slid down on loo seats, big trays, bin bags. Makeshift and man-made, the sledge-things cracked halfway down, on the sixth or tenth or twentieth go. When the snow thawed at last, I came for another walk, this time with a group of friends, because by then such things were permitted again. At the bottom of the hill there was a pile of broken, multicoloured plastic, washed up against the trees which marked the site where the smallpox hospital had stood briefly, before it was knocked down and the land returned to itself. Shards of sledge, abandoned to soak in the sun and meltwater. It should have been ugly, but I thought it was strange and beautiful. All that plastic would, I knew, be rotting in slow motion for tens of thousands of years. But I couldn't find it in me, that day, to regret it.

CHAPTER 6

Orkney

NO ADMITTANCE
—signs along the edge of Skara Brae,
West Mainland, Orkney

Flatlands seem to promise us a steady footing. We take this, as we often take our mothers, for granted. Both are expected to offer what the psychologist John Bowlby called the 'secure base,' a predictable environment on which one can build—a house, a city, a sense of self—and from which one can safely explore. For a baby to feel safe, the mother must hold it in a way that's unnoticeable: as a flatland holds a city, so convenient to its inhabitants that they never have to think about it.

When my mother asked for sanctuary in my grandmother's house in Scotland, tentatively, half my life ago, my grandmother didn't hesitate. She said yes, put down the phone, and went straight out to the charity shops to buy me a school uniform. Three days after we arrived, I was in class.

I'd always thought of myself as understanding Britain. I was half British, after all. I'd visited my grandmother for three months every second summer growing up: a small oasis of cool and magic in the middle of our lives. And I'd read Enid Blyton books, and Roald Dahl, and watched *Doctors* on my father's television, on the

BBC World Service. It turned out that Britain was neither like Enid Blyton nor like *Doctors*. The thing I remember most, absurdly, from those first few days, is the way the kids at school wore their ties in wide, fat knots. I couldn't take my eyes off them.

I knew it rained almost every day in Britain. I was ready for that. But I'd thought of gloves as a dated affectation, like parasols or petticoats. When winter came, I realized my mistake. The cold lit my fingerbones on fire from inside. Gloves were necessary. So were woolly hats, as though we were pictures of snowmen in children's books. My carrot nose ran with this wild cold, and I wiped it on my wrist.

There were so many rules. In Britain, for instance, you weren't meant to wear your coat inside the house. It was something you only put on when you ventured out, like a vulnerable little grub wrapping and unwrapping itself. It was a few years before I really noticed this rule. People had been too polite to make more than a passing comment when I wore my coat in class, or to friends' houses. It was a gigantic dark blue oilcloth affair that my grandmother had dug out of her attic. It made me look like a fisherman on a boat in a howling gale. It kept me dry, which as far as I was concerned was the whole point; I was too preoccupied to register it consciously as a point of difference from other people. But it was part of the cloud of unease I lived under. For the first two years in Scotland, walking around without a dupatta over my neck and chest, I felt agonizingly exposed.

'I wish I could wear a dupatta,' I said to my mother, in the kitchen. She put down the bowl in which she'd been washing rice, and gave me a hug.

'Don't hide your light under a bushel,' she said, quoting the Bible.

But other sorts of hiding seemed to be necessary. Loose clothing. High necklines. When I bought a lip tint for the first time, at the age of seventeen, disapproval radiated off my mother. When she caught sight of me hugging a male friend, she barely spoke to me for two days. The dupatta was an issue, I inferred, because it was Pakistani, was Muslim. The modesty underpinning it, on the other hand, was essential. After we left Pakistan, my mother receded fast from any explicit association with it, but the cultural norms she enforced were just the same.

My mother was born and raised in Fife, in a Church of Scotland family: austere and Presbyterian, emphasizing hard work, disapproving of frivolity. My grandmother taught biology at the local private school, which meant my mother got free tuition there. She tagged along as a day girl to a school so snobbish that it wouldn't let its students go into the local shops or even walk down the high street.

'My childhood was fine,' my mother said, opening the windows to let the air in. 'I was lonely, but lots of children are, aren't they? Generally I think your grandmother and I made a good team.'

Her father was depressed. He spent most of his evenings in bed. When my mother was thirteen, he killed himself. After a search, her seventeen-year-old brother found him hanging by his neck, in the garage.

'What did I feel when he killed himself?' my mother said, pulling laundry out of the machine. 'Nothing, to be honest. I think I felt: well, this doesn't make any difference. He'd already withdrawn from the family so completely.'

'Your mother's a saint,' my grandmother said, beaming at me. 'She would take your grandfather's food upstairs and just listen to him, patiently. I think she was the only one he felt he could talk to.'

My grandmother had always been busy: keeping the family going, teaching in school, raising the children. She'd teach anatomy with a pig's head in the morning, and have it on the stove at home by lunchtime, dissolving slowly into stock.

'When I was eight,' my mother said, proudly, emptying out the bin, 'I remember having a bad cold, and making a list of all the things I could do to feel better—have a hot drink, put a cold cloth on my head—before I disturbed your grandmother.'

'Your mother's always been very serious,' my grandmother said. 'Since she was a little girl.'

'I remember washing the gravel out of my own knees after I tripped and fell, rather than bother your grandmother when she was busy,' said my mother. 'I suppose I must have been around seven?'

'Your mother's always been very good,' my aunt—seven years older than my mother—said. 'That's the main thing I remember about her as a child. She was the good one.'

'Nothing happened to me,' my mother said.

'Your mother's a saint,' my grandmother said, again and again, as she shrank in her chair with throat cancer, and my mother patiently coaxed Ensure and banana into her.

It did seem that way. As my grandmother died, my mother slid ice chips between her parched lips, and lay on the floor by the bed in case she was needed in the night. She wouldn't let any of her daughters take a shift.

'I can go two nights without sleep,' she told us. 'It's only on the third night I start to struggle. So this is fine.'

It was the same in Pakistan. My mother grimly kept things going, kept us alive in an environment which was trying to kill us. Mosquitos, speeding cars, typhoid, violence, madness. Not one of us four, in eighteen years, got malaria, in a country to which it is endemic. None of us got typhoid or polio or dengue or hepatitis A. I remember my friends getting hepatitis: turning up to school after six weeks' absence, their eyeballs still yellow with jaundice. None of us died on the roads.

'Why didn't we leave before?' I'd asked my mother once. 'You knew things were wrong so early. You went into labour with Forget-Me-Not and he still made you make his lunch . . .'

She was hating this conversation. I was hating her for hating this conversation.

'I was worried that your father would get to keep you, under Islamic law. It was in your Islamiat textbook. The mother has the child till they are seven. And after that they belong to the father.'

'Did you ever check it with a lawyer?'

She looked vague.

'No.'

She had always avoided questions about *why*. Why she didn't protect my sisters and me. It seemed not to have occurred to her as a possibility.

'It wasn't as bad as all that, was it?' she said, when I pressed. 'I remember some very happy times. He had a temper, didn't he, but he never really beat any of us. He did fulfil—I suppose his basic parental duties. And if I needed money he'd usually give it to me.'

It was my mother's uncomplaining acceptance of suffering—for her, and by extension for us—which filled me with bewildered pain. I didn't understand how someone who loved me could think things in that house weren't bad, because that required seeing me as worthy of so little: no more than the thinnest basics of life.

Later she would tell me the story about Forget-Me-Not and the contractions and serving my father lunch again, and I thought I heard a note of pride in her voice.

After Pakistan, my mother pulled her life very small around her, like a mosquito net over a bed. Her main pleasures revolved around frugality. Bargains she'd found in the yellow-stickered section of the supermarket. Reusing something in an ingenious way. A tiny meal made out of leftovers. Talking to her could leave me feeling both miserable and frantic, half seduced by the prospect of a life shrunk almost to nothing and half desperate to escape it. We looked like each other, and we were so similar: a desire to move further and further towards a place where there was nothing. Once, in a rare confiding moment, I'd mentioned to my mother my recurring fantasy of buying a static caravan and eking out a small life there: my old dream of just hunkering down somewhere and waiting to die. Her eyes lit up.

'Come and live with me,' she said. 'We can wait together.'

It was alluring. It was deeply dangerous.

There was nothing to see in my mother—because nothing, she insisted, had happened to her either—but an intensity rose off her, like heat from a turned-off stove.

'It might not be relevant for your work any more, of course.' My mother's voice was uncertain on the phone. We hadn't spoken for a while. 'But if you were still thinking of going to Orkney for your research, and wanted company, then I'd love to come with you.'

It had been some years since I'd been back to Scotland—partly because of the coronavirus pandemic and partly because it was so painful. While I couldn't stop thinking of Pakistan, my mother seemed to have forgotten all about it.

But I found myself planning a joint trip with her, in the summer of 2022, to the islands of Orkney, where Neolithic standing stones jutted up into the sky, visible for miles. We would spend six days there, and already I could visualize myself ducking outside into the hostel bathroom to hyperventilate. Shouting at my mother. Crying. But at least, in that flat, remote landscape, there would be no hiding from each other.

I'd been busy in the previous months. I'd sold my flat in Newcastle, moved to Bristol—again, a city I'd never even visited before—and started my first permanent academic job, cramming myself and my things and Morvern into one short-term let after another. And Morvern had fallen ill. She'd been sick twice one weekend—a little popping mass of white bubbles, neatly, on the landlady's horrible cowhide rug, after which she resumed eating at speed—and I'd taken her to the vet on Monday, just in case. The vet shrugged. Morvern was a young cat. It was probably just one of those things. They offered to do her bloods just to put my mind at ease, and I said yes. The next morning they phoned me with orders to get her back in at once. Her kidneys were in failure, and there was no time to lose.

Morvern spent ten days in hospital. During that time, I did what turned out to be very right and important things. I phoned my friends and told them what was going on. I said yes when my best friend offered to come and stay. I curled my feet around hers on the landlady's big sofa, and talked about Morvern, and cried.

'I don't know why I'm crying,' I kept saying, between sobs. 'I'm not feeling sad. I'm okay. This is just something that's happening to my body.'

'You *are* feeling sad.' And my best friend looked terribly sad, too, sitting across from me, with a pillow on her lap. 'Your body knows you're feeling sad, even if you don't.'

All the same, it seemed strange and greedy to get kindness like this. My body was lying to everyone: weeping suddenly and forcefully without instructions from my brain. I told everyone this, but they went on being kind to me. And I began to feel better, and to understand that I would outlive Morvern; I would survive her death, and maybe even have another cat one day. All in all it was the most normal, most healing bad thing that had ever happened to me: something which people could understand, and with which they knew how to help. Ten days later Morvern came home, covered with shaven patches on her tummy and her legs and on the base of her tail. She gulped down her food as though she'd been starved, and jumped on every chair and shelf in direct contravention of vet's orders until I borrowed a crate to make her rest. Morvern looked up at me through the bars with real tears in her eyes. She might have another couple of years, if we were careful. I kissed her, breathing in the smell of the vet's surgery, seeking her own scent beneath it.

So things were stable, for now, amidst so much uncertainty. I'd arranged my life in a way that I could cope with. I didn't see many people. I certainly didn't speak to my sisters. When I woke up and asked myself, as I always did, 'Will I?'—will I go on, will I embark on another day?—the answer was consistently 'yes.' I got up and did another day, and sometimes without even noticing myself asking the question. I liked my little office, with its closed door: I hung a dupatta over the inside of the glass window, to make myself feel safe. I liked my colleagues and my students and my work. When I taught a seminar, I thought of nothing but poetry, and the faces in front of me, for its entire two hours.

So I feared the trip to Orkney. I was anxious about what might happen to Morvern while I was away. And I was terrified of the small, angry, petty person that I might become with my mother. Worse, I worried that my mother's view of things might topple me off-balance. It was very hard to want to be alive every day. My mother certainly didn't. She experienced the world as optional, and that was something I had inherited from her: the deep belief that I had the right to leave the party, just as soon as I had had enough.

It took me a whole day to get from Bristol to Scotland, seven hours with my laptop balanced on the curved bird-back of a folding plastic tray-table, hunching my shoulders in to take up less space. What I remembered most from travelling north in the past, when I was at university, was the way the sky and the landscape darkened and deepened as we moved into Scotland: it grew greener, more serious, more remote—from me, looking on, through the blue reflected window—and more lovely. But this time I was travelling along the west of England, and it felt different—it felt like nothing at all. The sun was shining and everything was very bright green. And there was no change from England to Scotland, not as far as I could see, as we crossed into the Lake District and then, suddenly, into Edinburgh Haymarket. Crossing the Forth into Fife, for the first time in three years, I pressed my face against the window and I thought maybe I felt something. And then we were at Leuchars, and my mother was on the platform, waiting for me.

'Do you want to look round the house?'

We were standing in the kitchen, which was cleaner and barer than I'd ever seen it. The big light cast deep shadows on the orange floor tiles. Forget-Me-Not was out at her supermarket shift.

'See if you can spot all the little changes.'

A newspaper cutting was pinned on the corkboard. 'Rangan's Tips: How you can feel great every day.'

RESPECT YOURSELF
TAKE A DAILY HOLIDAY
TALK TO STRANGERS
MAKE TIME FOR FRIENDS
SHUT DOWN DEVICES
CHOOSE A HAPPY STORY

I wandered through to the room that had been my grandmother's, and where she had died, four years ago. It was no longer a bedroom. My mother was trying to give it a new identity, to drive out the ghosts. Now there were two armchairs—one which converted into a single bed—and a recliner chair in black leather. All three faced the same way, with a small multicoloured rug spread out in front of them.

'What do you think of the black chair?' My mother had appeared behind me. 'I got it for free! Someone at the end of the road was giving it away!'

'It's great, Wol.'

I'd called her Wol, like the owl from *Winnie-the-Pooh*, since I was a teenager, because it made me nervous to call her Amma or Mum. Mothering and being mothered felt very complicated. It was better to play a game which wasn't quite a game.

'I put it together myself,' my mother said. 'It's harder than it looks!'

'I bet it would be.'

There was a new desk in the spare room where me and my sisters slept when we visited.

'Have you got slippers for the hostel?' My mum poked her head in again.

'Ah. I don't. I thought about bringing some, actually, but then it went out of my head.'

'They'll want you to have slippers. I'll find some you can borrow.' Her head vanished.

I sat down on the little cabin bed. It was coming on 8 p.m., but still as light outside as four in the afternoon.

My mother came back in with her hands full. 'So I've got some options for you. These—' she held up a little floral pocket—'were your grandmother's—'

I interrupted her before she could introduce the next pair, taking the pocket and sliding out the folded slippers. Navy blue, decorated with orange flowers and turquoise swirls, and folded down to the size of a smartphone. 'Did she use them?'

'I think so. She kept them in her overnight bag, for when she had to go into hospital.'

The cream-coloured inner soles had discoloured to orange at the places where the heel and the ball of the foot would apply pressure. 'These are great. Would anyone mind if I had these?'

'Not at all. I don't think anyone else knows they exist.'

I hooked one of my dead grandmother's slippers onto my foot, and stuck it out in front of me.

'You keep them. They're yours now.'

Because Morvern had been so ill, my mother hadn't quite believed—she told me later, on the train to Aberdeen—that the trip would go ahead, until she saw me standing there at Leuchars station.

'How exciting,' she kept saying, as we pulled our cases through Aberdeen, heading to the ferry terminal. The sun was shining, and the city's strange turreted buildings stood out grey against the blue, like a chunky Playmobil fairy tale.

Most of the flat landscapes I'd visited—Orford Ness, the fens, Morecambe Bay—were spaces around water, or where water had been pulled back—and was still held back—by force. Orkney is a little different. Four hundred million years ago, what is now Orkney was part of the Orcadian Basin—a large depression in the earth— together with what is now Caithness in Northern Scotland, and little bits of Shetland.

Over time, the basin filled with water and became Lake Orcadie. As millions of years passed, sediment was deposited and compacted in this lake, making layers of flat flagstones, and those thin, level layers of sedimentary rock became the low-lying landscapes of modern Orkney. Pieces of the same flat rock lie everywhere on Orkney's beaches today. They've been used for building on the islands for centuries, or levered up from the ground and set on end to become standing stones.

Back when Orkney's seventy islands were all part of the basin, and before that a tiny, tiny part of the vast Pangea supercontinent, they sat near the equator. Desert winds blew, and it was as hot as sub-Saharan Africa today. It was only later that these areas of land would migrate north and separate out into the pieces scattered away from mainland Scotland.

This is one creation story for Orkney—the one geologists tell. But there are others. Tom Muir's *Orkney Folk Tales* tell of the Stoor Worm, whose flat incisors were knocked out in its death throes, falling into the sea and becoming the islands of Orkney. And of the giant who went to Norway to cut peats; he stopped for a gigantic shit on the way back, which became *Shet* (or *shit*) land, and dropped all his peats when his basket broke, and the peats became Orkney.

Six hours, on the ferry from Aberdeen to Orkney. The sea was like mud: brown mud when the sun flashes on it and turns it silver-grey, rucked up into rims by bootheels. The water gathered into a pinch and pushed backwards; the ship sighed and spat out foam.

A gannet flew alongside the ferry for a while, its head yellowed as though by accident: brushed with turmeric or aged like paper. It flew very straight and seriously, its big body close to the window, and I had a strong sense of it as a living thing, an animal, held aloft by its muscles: a thick, sweet potato, double handful of bird, choosing to move through the air beside us. Beyond, someone had dropped the sun on the sea, like spilt milk. I put my head on the window.

'There's land,' I said suddenly, surprising myself awake. Barely, through the darkening evening, there was land. One little nub, and a streak like a tadpole on the top of the sea. The window was blurred by a dash of rain, but the land kept coming, in a long unspooling line. It barely broke out of the sea, this island, keeping a level just above the water. And it was so flat that if you let your eyes lose focus, it vanished back into the waves. My heart started beating in my throat. As we moved closer, the island thickened, sharp at the edge like a biscuit stamped out by a cutter, but still flat on top. I wanted to snap off a piece with my teeth and feel it on my tongue.

We went out onto the viewing deck, where men were smoking and two girls were singing with their arms around each other's waists. And more of the islands started sliding into view: dark and rocky, green and plush, on either side of us. Between them, the ship left a broad streaked-white path, vanishing off into the blue horizon.

We were staying on Mainland for the whole trip—the biggest island in the archipelago—at a youth hostel in Kirkwall. Our plan was to do everything by public transport; I hadn't managed to pass my driving test, and my mother was less and less confident behind the wheel as the years went on. What I hadn't anticipated was just how few buses there would be once we got to Orkney. In particular there seemed to be almost none from Kirkwall to Skara Brae, the famous Neolithic settlement on the west side of the island. When I put the journey into Google Maps, our first night in the hostel, there seemed only to be one bus, which turned straight round as soon as it arrived and left again.

We lay in our single beds, and considered the problem.

'Another option,' I said into the dark, staring straight up, 'might be hiring bikes.'

'Ah,' my mother said, injecting the syllable with all the doubt it could hold. 'I'm not sure about that.'

I had expected this. 'Are you worried about the gradient? Or about staying on? It's very flat.'

'No, darling, it's just that I haven't ridden a bike for decades.'

'They say you never forget,' I said absently, already moving on in my mind, knowing she wouldn't agree.

'I don't think it's a good idea.'

A pause.

'Or we could hire a car,' I said. 'Or take a taxi.'

'Do *we* really need to go to Skara Brae?'

'Wol—' I sat up, exasperated. 'Yes, we do. We've come all this way. It would be *stupid* to come all the way to Orkney and not go to Skara Brae.'

'It's just that I'll enjoy whatever we do. Even in the simplest walk there's something to look at and enjoy.'

A ball of irrational wire rage was rolling into me, hard. 'Listen, this is probably the only time in our lives we're going to come to Orkney. It would be a *waste* not to go.'

'All right. I'm just saying that I really don't mind.'

My mother: lapsing into inertia for the price of a taxi fare, for the sake of the effort it might take to try something new. How did one live in the midst of this extreme passivity? If all things were equal, what were we even doing here? Why weren't we lying on our living-room floors, watching the dance of the dust, today and every day? I turned towards the wall and pulled the thin edges of my duvet around me.

The next morning I woke up, determined that things would be better. We went to the bakery and ordered fried egg rolls—I added a potato scone and cheese to mine, with stubborn greed—which we ate near the cathedral. My mother was very drawn by the town hall opposite, with its small turrets and figures over the door. 'Will you take a photo?' she said. 'I want to look up what those statues are, later.'

Everything was as interesting as everything else. When my mother couldn't think of anything to say, she started reading the business signs as we went past. 'BBC Radio Orkney! Virgin Money!' She inspected a contactless charity donation point in a window with all the curiosity of a prisoner on day release for the first time in twenty years. She exclaimed over a swirling Celtic mural on the side of a building which turned out to be an advertisement for Highland Park whisky. 'Noreen, look—'

It was a display of brightly coloured chocolate bars, in a shop.

'You could take a lovely photo even of that, couldn't you?'

We had ten minutes before the tourist information centre opened, and I spotted a sign for a craft fair. The first stall displayed sea glass and sea china that had been turned into earrings and brooches and pictures. My mother was entranced.

'That one's beautiful.' She was pointing at a seascape, with a boat made out of sea glass, the sea made of curls of cloth. 'I wonder about getting it.'

'I'll buy it for you!' I blurted out. What a chance—how often did my mother ever express a desire for something? 'For your birthday!'

To my amazement, my mother assented. The stallholder slid it into a brown paper bag, and invited us to pick out a little piece of free sea glass from a bowl with a heart painted on it.

'I'm looking for flat landscapes,' I said to her. 'Are there any parts of Mainland you'd recommend?'

She laughed. 'It's all flat!'

At another stall, the lady was knitting. 'Good morning, ladies.' By the laptop in front of her there lay a small golliwog toy. In one glance I could see that it had nothing to do with anything she was selling. She'd put it there just because she could.

I turned away without saying a word, and started chatting to the next stallholder. Later I mentioned it to my mother, in a low voice, as we stepped out of the building. She hadn't noticed it, but she agreed with me.

'It's not really okay, is it.' I could hear her working through the idea as she spoke. 'Even if it's something you're fond of—from when you were a child—you don't bring it and put it on your stall like that.'

'Exactly,' I said. The brown paper bag, holding her gift, dangled from my hand.

In the tourist information centre, a kind young man explained that there was, in fact, a functioning bus to Skara Brae: it went on Mondays, Thursdays and Saturdays. So that was all right: we could go tomorrow. One problem solved.

'I'm looking for really flat landscapes,' I said. 'Are there any really flat parts of Mainland, or any of the other islands, that you'd recommend?'

'It's all flat!' The young man beamed.

'I know,' I said. 'But maybe there are some really flat bits you know of?'

He was showing me, with a rod on his big map, where the flattest parts of Mainland were, when my mother suddenly spoke up.

'What about the Italian Chapel?' she asked. 'I'd like to go there.'
And she gestured to a rack of postcards.

I was astonished. It was so rare for my mother to express a
preference; now she'd done it twice in twenty minutes. I'd never
heard of the Italian Chapel, but I seized it with both hands.

'Yes! We absolutely can go to the Italian Chapel! Let's go now!'

Later, on the bus, my mother asked me, 'You don't mind me pointing things out to you, do you?'

'No, not at all,' I said. 'Just, sometimes I might not answer. Like,
if I'm concentrating. It takes me a while to really . . . sink into things,
and be with them.'

It was a relief to say this aloud, and a relief that she seemed to
understand.

'Almost like meditation,' my mother said.

The Italian Chapel was on the east of Mainland. It had been a
Nissen hut, during the Second World War, and Italian prisoners
of war had converted it into a place of worship. From the outside
it lay like a barrel on its side, undeniably barrack-shaped. But inside they had gone to great lengths to turn its plasterboard walls
into three dimensions. They'd painted bricks, columns, intricately
carved stonework. All flat, but with the illusion of depth, painted
shadows marshalled carefully in the grooves of the painted carvings.
The prisoners had made lanterns out of the remains of a ship, and
they dangled from the ceiling.

'Amazing,' said my mother. 'They just did their best with
what they had.'

Perhaps this was why my mother had been drawn to the Italian Chapel, I thought. The theme of making do, the best of a bad job, doing what you could with what you had. The thought tasted sour. I wanted my mother to like things because they were beautiful and fun, not because they were practical or efficient. Even at thirty-two years old, I had a primitive, hot need inside me: I wanted my mother to show me how to enjoy being alive.

'Tell me again where you met Aba?' I asked her. We were waiting for the bus, in the path of a sharp wind.

'Bradford,' my mother said. 'He was doing a registrar's post at the time. We met a few times, and he took me out to dinner.'

'And he brought you carnations,' I supplied.

'Yes. He brought me carnations, once. That was sweet. He was quite exotic-looking, I suppose. He always wore a tie, even when we went on hikes. Very smart Western clothes.'

'And then you slept together,' I said, baldly.

'Yes,' my mother said. 'That was a strange situation. In his bedroom. He got in front of the door, and I couldn't get out.'

There was a silence.

'And so it was felt that we should probably get married. That's how things were, at the time, if you'd been physically intimate.'

Norse mythology is full of tales of giants living out in the wilderness. This works fine in mountainous Scandinavia, but the myths faltered when they arrived in Orkney: How could anyone believe that giants were hiding somewhere in this flat landscape? So the stories about giants on Orkney became fables about what happens when you leave yourself exposed. One night a group of giants gathered to dance and they became so caught up in the music that they failed to notice the sun rising. And as its rays lit them up, they were all turned to stone: the standing stones still visible today, tall and stark on the silent fields of Orkney.

There are two major groups of standing stones on Mainland: the Stones of Stenness and the bigger Ring of Brodgar. As it happened, I'd been to see Stonehenge, their more famous southern cousin, the week before: on a bus packed with tourists, with plastic orange headphones which plugged into the seat in front of you. You could only see the henge from a distance, through a crowd of picnickers, while the rooks perched on the lintel stones and squirted white trails down the sides.

The Stones of Stenness were even older than Stonehenge. We made the trip out to see them on our first day, after we'd finished in the chapel. From the bus they were a small gathering of shards, fanning impossibly upwards from the surface of the earth. When we arrived there was no one else there. No fence or barricade or ticket booth. Just some sheep, staring mildly, and a folding blackboard advertising a free guided tour at 10 a.m. And beyond, a sky ridged with dark grey.

The grey stones stood like huge, gentle, awkward men, wide-shouldered, hunching round slightly, who had lost their arms somewhere. Three tall ones, and a jaunty small one which changed direction halfway along its length, bending the other way to make a corner. One of the myths which hangs over Orkney is that the standing stones leave their places at Hogmanay and go down to the loch to drink. I could see, in my mind, the kind, worried stones twisting their big shoulders right down, with great difficulty, to try to get their mouths to the water level for a sip.

I walked up to the first standing stone. My mother had found a bird to look at in the nearby loch and hadn't caught up yet. The stones were pitted with the acid of rain, their pockets full of yellow lichen, right to the top, far over my head. I put my face against the cold dry surface and closed my eyes. From the side this stone was almost fragile, its layers worn unevenly away. As though it only kept standing through great effort, on the green field which stretched away in all directions, for thousands of years.

Another stone lay flat on the ground, with smaller stones balanced upright nearby. The quiet was complete. Little wisps of sheep wool had caught in the cracks and scars of the rock; they fluttered in the wind. Outside the stone field, the grass flowed and rippled, shining like clean hair.

What are Britain's stone circles for? They were used for ritual purposes. That's an old archaeologist's joke. If you don't know what a monument or artefact was for, you say it had ritual purposes. Looking at my mother's Orkney guidebook, though, I kept thinking of a tweet I'd seen, saying that if an archaeologist dug up Disneyland, they would without hesitation classify it as a religious site. We use such poor, narrow, clumsy categories to try and grasp the unknown. Difference is difficult to truly imagine. Who says that the stone circles were even monuments at all? The archaeologist Colin Richards suggests: 'Rather than being built solely as ritual or ceremonial centres it may have been the actual acts of construction that provided the main social focus.' People would have gathered to watch and participate, with stones perhaps being added slowly over time. Perhaps it was the type of stones that mattered: maybe they were from a sacred place. Perhaps the point was not a symbolic ring to unify society, but a competitive process of quarrying and transportation.

It's one mental step to establish that people in the past—or in other countries—were or are 'just like us.' That's an easy act of generosity which is really more like narcissism. It's quite another thing to grasp that their thinking, their priorities, their assumptions, might be utterly different from ours: unimaginable and unreachable. And yet at the same time—this is the leap—to understand viscerally that they were still just as human. Our own minds are not the measure of what is worthwhile.

When we were back in the hostel room, my phone buzzed. It was my housemate, sending the pictures of Morvern he'd promised me. She was sitting on a bench in the kitchen, looking aggravated and vacant, and I laughed aloud.

'Dear, dear Morvern!' my mother exclaimed, when I showed her. 'So much personality. And so beautiful. She really is a very special cat.'

This was another way that my mother was like me. She found it easiest, by far, to show love to animals.

I started sorting through the day's photographs. 'Are you hungry?' I said absently, tapping out notes on my phone. 'I can do this later. We can start dinner.'

'No, I'm fine,' my mother said. But five minutes later she'd fished some crisps out of my backpack and was munching. I was so pleased. She'd encountered a need in herself, and she'd met it: as though she were daring to be a human in front of me. As the trip went on, I saw her eating more and more, and I started to relax.

My mother liked the hostel very much. She spent the evening scavenging through the 'free stuff' shelf in the kitchen: half a loaf of brown sourdough, some leftover sliced cheese and some blueberries made their way into our stash. Even a half jar of peanut butter, lined up next to the full jar we had already bought.

'Perhaps we should leave it on the shelf,' I said diplomatically, over dinner. 'It won't go off, and someone else might like to use it. We don't really need two jars of peanut butter.'

My mother returned the peanut butter to the free shelf without complaint, and went back to asking everyone in the dining room about themselves. I could hear her voice piping up, here and there, as I typed.

The next morning, we set out to climb Wideford Hill: the highest point on this mostly flat island. On the way up, my mother told me about all the people she'd met in the dining room last night.

'And the woman from Shropshire,' my mother said, 'this is her second night up. And she was telling me how she lived in Australia for two years.'

'Do you think we take a left here?' I wasn't interested in this woman I'd never met.

'Her son's on the autism spectrum. Partly in mainstream school and partly in—you know, in a special school. But he's very good at maths. She's really made the most of his education. And he actually has no problems with socialization, strangely enough.'

There were huge orange poppies in groups everywhere, leaving their loose petals on the ground like damp towels, some edged with white in their creases where they'd outgrown their own colour. In among the flowers were the big oval buds, the flower packed up tight inside with just a bit of orange crepe showing at the top. I stopped to hold one in my hand, gently, then tightly, like the nub of a small, curled-up fist. It fitted perfectly and withstood my grip. I liked it so much that I stopped again, later, and held another. My mother said nothing, and I was grateful.

I noticed as we climbed that I was leaving my mother behind. This was new. Normally she stormed single-mindedly ahead. Now she was moving carefully behind me, walking with her pole stuck out at a strange angle. As we climbed, Kirkwall bent and sank below us. Over on the sea I could see the oil rig standing. On the horizon, more and more islands unfolded.

At the top of the hill, I climbed up on a little mound and looked down, hands on my hips. 'Well,' I said. I was disappointed. What the hill view showed us was the number of other little hills: the unflatness of Mainland, as it rose and fell in distinct undulations around us. I started going down the hill again.

'I'm just going to—' I turned round, and my mother was bustling to the other side of the summit, to look from that angle. So completist, I thought resignedly. After a moment or two I followed her.

'Is that a fish farm?' my mother said. Eight little grey rounds were linked together on the sea, like the plastic rings that hold beer cans together. And beyond—I suddenly noticed—was an island which looked much flatter than Mainland. What was it?

We puzzled together over the silver compass map on a plinth—installed, it told us, by the Rotary Club—and worked out that the flat island was Shapinsay. Encouraged, I went a little farther over, towards the edge of the hill. And there, below, were two perfect islands. Rounded and flat and thin, like water biscuits, like patches of green suede on a grey-glittering sea. They just, just held themselves up over the sea—level, from this distance, with its meniscus.

'Thank you for checking the other side!' I said to my mum, as we made our way back down Wideford Hill. 'If you hadn't, we wouldn't have seen all these amazing islands! And they look so good from above!'

She looked pleased. 'It was worth it, wasn't it? Just to get that view. That overview.'

Using Google Maps, I worked out what the tiny flat islands were. The Holm of Grimbister, and Damsay. Damsay was uninhabited. The Holm of Grimbister had a causeway which appeared at low tide, so you could walk over to it. Its highest point—I could hardly believe it—was just eight metres above sea level. Eight metres! I was gripped. From that moment I was determined to get myself to the Holm of Grimbister: sixteen hectares, population of three.

Despite its general flatness, many strange mounds dot the Orkney landscape. Some of these are natural glacial deposits. Some are artificial, covering Neolithic chambered tombs, or Iron Age 'brochs': magnificent stone roundhouses. Fairies are said to live in these mounds, with the power to steal your babies or your horses if you disturb them.

At Skara Brae, when we finally got there, ten perfectly preserved neolithic dwellings sank into the ground, each with the same furniture: two bed boxes, made out of propped-up stones, and a stone dresser. The grass made figures-of-eight atop the stacked stone walls, each house nesting into its neighbour. They had no roofs, and you could look straight down from above into the neat, tight living quarters. But the seventh house was just a brown mound, scattered with tufts of grass.

House 7 contains the best preserved stone carvings found at Skara Brae. It was fitted in 1929 with a shielding glass roof, but studies revealed that this was creating temperature changes that caused the carvings to flake and crumble. In 2005 the decision was made to re-roof the building in turf.

I stared at the blank brown mound for a long time, before I moved on to the other dwellings. In the grass, by every house entrance, small signs read NO ADMITTANCE. This far: no farther. Under the hot blue sky, the green fields stretched far and flat around us.

On the beach by Skara Brae there were a handful of limpet shells; a crab claw, jewelled in purple beads; a feather here and there; and about fifteen dead birds. Gannets, with their turmeric-brushed heads.

'A shame,' my mother said. She went right up to one bird, as I would have done—unperturbed by death and decay—and peered at it.

Some of the birds were eaten right down to the skull, ribcage standing open like a hull. Some were very fresh and almost intact. All of them had lost their upturned eye; the swarming flies always started there.

'We're getting this on the east coast too,' said my mum. 'So many dead birds on the beaches. It's bird flu. So odd that it's here too. Dreadful.'

Even in the most rotten bodies, the bones still held together with a tangle of wiry tendons, with honeycombed dry flesh. I left them there on the beach. I picked up the bleached sea branches, white as hair, and dropped them again.

Our Skara Brae tickets also gave us admission to Skaill House, a seventeenth-century mansion nearby. A little bird hopped over the grass outside the house, pale belly, dark wings, about the size of a sparrow, but slender. I pointed it out to my mother, just before it flew away.

Inside, small, ugly, expensive things were arranged on side tables and behind velvet ropes. A white tiger had been turned into a skin, crudely edged with red fabric, and spread over the floor. *Acquired by the present Laird's grandfather, Robert Scarth Farquhar Macrae, while serving as Inspector General of Police in Behar and Orissa, India.* There was a little cabinet of game pieces from China, and a Japanese carving. People crammed into the house, too many, peering at the cases, murmuring respectfully.

I sped through, leaving my mother behind without a word, bumping in my haste into people's backpacks, and waited in the gift shop.

'I'm here,' I said, as I saw her coming down the stairs. I was conscious of having perhaps been rude.

'Hello.'

I couldn't tell if she was annoyed.

'Would you like an ice cream?' my mother said.

'Um. Would you like one?'

'Would *you* like an ice cream?'

I chose raspberry.

'You go ahead and wait outside. I'll just be a minute.'

Somehow, it seemed, my mother had picked up on how I was feeling. This broke all my rules. She wasn't allowed to know how I felt; that never ended well, for me or for her. But something about this quiet, tactful knowing made me malleable. I went outside and crouched down outside the door, crossing my arms over my knees and putting my face down on the sun-warmed skin.

My mother appeared with two ice creams.

'Was it a bit suffocating in there?' she asked. To my horror, I felt myself starting to cry.

We sat down on the edge of a wall, and I slung my legs over, weeping into my wrist, holding my little tub of ice cream with the other hand.

'Oh, sweetheart,' I heard my mother say, quietly.

'It's evil,' I said inanely into the arm of my T-shirt. 'Rich people are so boring. That's the worst of it. Rich white people. They're so boring, and yet they're the only ones we ever hear about. They can be totally, totally banal, and everyone else—all the rest of the world— just has to give in and listen politely.'

My mother touched my shoulder and rocked it a little. Gradually I stopped crying, and levered up an edge of melting ice cream with my little plastic spoon. We sat in silence for a while.

'I feel like I'm boring too,' said my mother. Was that dampness, in the dark curve under her eye?

'Sorry,' I said dully. 'I didn't mean that all white people are boring. I don't think you're boring.'

'No, not that. I know. *I* think I'm particularly boring. I don't have anything to say or contribute. I don't know what I have to offer.'

'It's so weird to me that you think that.' I scooped up the last of the ice cream, dropped the spoon into the tub and crushed it between both palms. 'You've had such an interesting life! You moved to another country—you converted to another religion!'

'I just feel that my life in Pakistan was so empty,' my mother said. 'There's nothing to say about it. Nothing to talk about.'

It was a problem.

'I remember you saying, when we were in Lahore'—I chose my words carefully—'that your plan was to stop eating one day, when no one needed you, and just wait to die.'

'Yes,' my mother said. 'That feeling never really goes away.'

'That's not okay, Wol. It's not something you should just have to live with.'

'Hmm,' my mother said. She took off her glasses and swiped the tears away. 'Sorry. Competitive crying is awful.'

'It's fine.' I patted her tentatively on the elbow.

It was a short while before I spoke again. 'Sometimes I feel like you're proudest of me—not when I do something impressive, or get a job or publish a paper, or anything like that—but when I make myself smaller. Like when I do a task efficiently, or reuse something round the house.'

'I'm so proud of you,' said my mother. 'I can't believe you don't know that. I'm so proud of you.'

Tears were spilling out of me again.

'I just feel so inadequate,' my mother said.

'I don't want you to feel inadequate,' I said. 'That's why I don't tell you stuff.' I picked at my boot, where the brown fabric on the upper was beginning to come away from the dark stuffing. 'We're a terrible family for comparing ourselves to each other.'

My mother laughed. 'Yes. We are.'

I was feeling soothed. It had been a long time since my mother had been able to soothe me. Even so, it took me a few moments before I could bring it up from deep in my throat.

'I love you,' I said gruffly, staring out at the beach.

'I love you too. So much. Thank you. That means a lot.'

'I'm just bad at attachment,' I said, with wooden absurdity.

'I know,' said my mother.

I digested that for a moment.

The little bird we had seen before—dark wings, pale tummy— hopped back into view. I pointed it out, and my mother rummaged for her binoculars, and just as she brought them out, the little bird flew away. I looked it up later, on the RSPB bird identifier. It could have been a red-backed shrike. Or it could have been almost anything else.

I couldn't stop thinking about the Holm of Grimbister, float- ing like a communion wafer on the blue water. Dimensionless. I looked on Google Maps and found a garage on Mainland which sat nearly parallel with the Holm. The next morning I phoned them up, listening to the ringing while my boiled egg went cold in its slick of margarine.

'I'm so sorry to bother you,' I said, when a man picked up. 'I know this is an odd question. I'm writing a book about flat landscapes, and I'm trying to get to the Holm of Grimbister. I don't suppose there are any local fishermen around who might be able to take me across?'

'No fishermen around here any more,' the man said dolefully.

'Ah. I'm sorry.' There was an awkward moment of silence, for the gone fishermen. 'Could you tell me—how long is the causeway visible at low tide?'

The man thought it would be about an hour, either side. 'But if it isn't,' he added merrily, 'it's a nice day for a swim!'

I was encouraged. 'It's not shallow enough to wade, is it? At higher tide?'

'Only if you've got very long legs!'

We laughed, and I hung up, feeling warm and fizzy. We'd be able to get there tomorrow. But first, Shapinsay.

When we arrived, though, Shapinsay—which had looked so flat from Wideford Hill—turned out to have a hill of its own. We agreed to climb Ward Hill, identify the flat parts of the island from above, and make our way down to them.

'The other end of the island's particularly flat,' said the lady in the Shapinsay shop. 'But if you've only got two hours, you won't have time to go all the way there.' She considered the tourist information map spread between us on the counter. 'Unless you hire e-bikes.'

I looked resignedly at my mother, who gave her head a tight shake, eyes half closed.

'Sorry,' I said to the lady. 'I think e-bikes are a great idea, but my mum's not so sure.'

'I haven't ridden a bike in decades,' my mother repeated.

'Well, it's not just bikes,' the lady said. 'They have a tricycle you could hire, if you're worried about falling off. It's very easy to ride them.'

My mother coughed and looked away, but I leaned over the counter while she gave me directions to the bike hire.

'We'll just go and have a look,' I said as we left the shop, moving with purpose along the road. My mother was coughing with alarm, walking obediently alongside me, trying to find a reason not to hire a bike.

'But you're meant to do a flat *walk*,' she said. 'Not a flat *bike ride*. It's not the same thing. A completely different experience.'

'Wol, if you're scared, just say so.'

'Hahaha,' she said darkly, and fell silent.

At the e-bike hire, my mother was cheered to discover that all the bikes had been booked already.

'But you're welcome to try them out just now!' the shop owner added. The smile vanished from my mother's face.

'Try the tricycle!' I said. 'Honestly, you couldn't be safer. You won't need to balance.'

'You first,' my mother said, holding on to her money belt with both hands. I struggled to mount it.

'I find the tricycle much harder than the bikes,' the shop owner said, as one after the other we blundered a few inches forward. 'It's harder to control.'

'I'll try the bike, then!' I said brightly, climbing on. 'And then you, Wol!'

'Well,' my mother said.

I rode the bike round in a clumsy circle, laughing as it lurched up on to the verge.

'Now you!' I said, swinging my leg off and holding out the handlebars to her. And to my surprise, my mother did mount it.

'You can go across the road to that driveway,' said the owner. 'Give yourself some space.'

In the driveway, my mother pushed off and froze, wobbling dangerously, with her feet unmoving on the pedals.

'Use the pedals!' I called. She juddered to a halt and caught herself with one foot.

'You can do it! Push off again!' And she did.

'Left foot down! Push!' To my amazement, after one long, agonizing second, the left pedal went down, and the bike stabilized.

'Right foot down! Left foot! Right! You're doing it!'

My mother was riding a bike, for the first time in nearly fifty years. I cheered and clapped. Grinning, we returned over the road and handed the bike back.

'I'm so glad you did that! Thank you!' I clung to her arm in a half hug, as we walked away.

'I could even try riding a bike at home now!' my mother said. 'It wasn't as hard as I thought it was going to be!'

The climb up Ward Hill was long but gentle. On the horizon, towards the sea, I could see what looked like a tall figure in black, with a white bib. It was too still to be anything but a post or a mast, but it entered my head fully formed as a beautiful girl looking out to sea. I could see her very clearly in my mind. Her face was made of polished wood, the pale grain circles rounding out from a centre offset on one cheek. She had no arms, and at her ankles her skirt flared. She was waiting for me.

When I reached the top, the wind was blowing hard. Beside me, a turbine roared. I pulled myself up on to the painted platform with some difficulty, and it was a few moments before my mother appeared as well.

'What do you think?' she asked, when we'd peered for a while over the green swells below us.

'I suppose that's the flattest bit, over there,' I said, pointing towards a sandy cove which bit into the green, barred with the shine of water. It still wasn't very flat, though. I felt worried.

'Shall we head there?'

I hopped off the viewing platform, but stopped when my mother said, 'Noreen . . .' I turned round, and she was holding out her hand to me. I took it and guided her down. That was the first time she'd ever asked for my help.

There wasn't time to go far before we had to return for the ferry, but we headed down the hill towards the bay, past a field of brown cows who ran up to the fence to glare at us. My mother lagged behind, but whenever I turned round she was clutching the chest strap of her backpack and smiling at the scenery, so I headed on at my own pace.

We reached the edge of the cove. 'Do you think your boots will be okay?' I asked.

'I think so.'

I took a step out onto it. Firm sand, stained dark blue and patterned with the coiled lengths that meant lugworms, with just a thin layer of water spread over the top. You could walk safely on land like that. From a distance it looked like it might give way beneath you, but in the end it would hold you up. I walked over the whole bay: where green seaweed made a bubbled crunch underfoot, where the water under my boots made a sound like one hand patting the other. My mother followed behind, very slowly.

As we reached the other side of the sand, the green heaped up into a thick, round-edged layer, like combed fondant. Pink-white flowers, stiff-petalled, grew on the saline sand.

'I think that's thrift,' my mother said.

We sat down in the grass which blew all around us. From here, Ward Hill looked like nothing. There was the dark green layer of the vegetation around us, then the thin brown sliver of bay; an apple-green bank beyond which was the hill, and a vast blue sky above. The wind blew the grassy tussocks around like messy heads of hair. The horizon beyond held nothing to hurt us.

Heading back to the harbour, I saw long tail feathers and downy fluff gathered in the grass. I stooped down and picked a whole sternum out of the grass, with spiky bits of rib fanning out on both sides, and the loop of the collarbone intact. It looked, I thought, like some kind of Neolithic plough. I picked two long wing bones out of the grass too—there was no time to scout for the skull—and caught up with my mother, who had stopped to watch.

'Bones,' I said, showing her.

'Ah,' said my mother. 'Will you be taking them with you?'

'Yes.'

'What are you going to do with them?'

'I collect bones,' I said.

'Ah.' She thought for a moment. 'Do you want to put them in my pink foldaway bag?'

I did.

———

'When did you start feeling that you could just stop eating one day?' I asked my mother as we made our way towards the ferry.

She thought. 'I think it was worst in Pakistan. None of us were eating very much, were we? And I thought: What's the point? A great feeling of emptiness.'

'Yes.' I watched her to see if she would say anything else. 'So it was worst in Pakistan. But when did it first start? Do you remember?'

'I was very depressed after my undergrad,' my mother said. 'And no one was any help.'

'You asked for help?' I was astonished. This didn't sound like my mother at all. 'Who did you go to see?'

'The psychiatrist. He stripped me naked to examine me, and then gave me Diazepam.' There was a pause. 'It was very shaming. And it didn't help at all.'

The thought was so terrible I could barely finish thinking it. This was all new information. 'That's awful. Really awful. They'd never do that today.'

'I know,' my mother said.

There was a pause. 'You're glad we left Pakistan, aren't you?'

'Certainly for me it was the best thing,' my mother said. 'Though I was sad my marriage had failed. I did hope, right up until the end, that we could all be a happy family.'

She seemed about to say something else, but suddenly broke off. 'What's that bird?' There was a long creaking noise, and I looked over to the side. A bird's head was poking out of a patch of tall grass.

'Corncrake!' I pointed it out to her.

'Yes!' My mother was jubilant. 'How wonderful!'

'I think there's another there too!'

We watched the two birds for a while, and then moved on. 'That's made my day,' my mother said.

Later she said it again: 'That was my favourite part of the day.'

I was glad I had found it for her.

'There are three doors into any person,' my friend Cobes said to me once. She was training to be a therapist. 'The feelings door, the thoughts door, and the actions door. Often people don't know what they're feeling. So you can ask them what they're thinking. Or even: What do you *think* you're feeling?'

'What did you feel when my father died?' I asked my mother now. 'Do you remember?'

'Fine, really,' my mother said. 'Nothing in particular.'

No admittance. This far: no farther.

I waited a few hours, until we were eating dinner together, and then tried again. 'What do you *think* you felt, when Aba died?'

Now my mother paused for a long time, chewing. 'I remember that my eyes were wet, when I woke up the next day,' she said. 'So I must have felt sad, I suppose.'

On the map in the hostel reception, the Holm of Grimbister was surrounded by a frill of rocks in the eggshell-blue sea; this touched, just, a second frill of rocks which hooked out into the sea from Holm Point. On Google Maps the island was more mysterious. The red pin sat in the middle of the sea, and a little dotted line ran out to it from the shore. A plunge into the unknown. As we rounded past Wideford Hill on the bus, and the islands floated into sight, I strained without success to see any signs of the causeway. It was still submerged.

We'd researched the tide times the night before. Different websites said different times: the earliest was 13.05, the latest was 14.55. If we arrived an hour ahead of the earliest possible time, I reasoned, that should guarantee us getting on the island. We just might have to wait for a while. Maybe for a long while.

'It might do,' my mother said. 'Perhaps.' She was very unsure about the whole thing.

On the side of the road, staring towards the island, I scanned the field in front of us, where some rhubarb had escaped over the neighbouring garden wall and was rampaging outwards into the field with huge reckless leaves. How did one even get on the causeway? I led us down a driveway, past a squashed hedgehog with its insides showing wet like raspberry filling, towards a tarmac slope into the sea where a yellow boat perched. A slate beach edged the cliffs round. Bladdered seaweed heaped up in huge, stiff piles; little sprays of weed made small posies on the wide flat rocks. At points, the slates fitted together like square tiles.

At the causeway, my mother said nervously, 'Don't go out onto it yet.' Most of the track was still underwater, but seaweed was starting to show through in an outline which traced where the path would rise up through the water. We climbed up off the beach and made our way along the unpaved road, where cars charged fast towards their destinations, into Finstown, where we found a teashop and enquired, once again, about low tide. No one seemed to know. A few people guessed, unhelpfully.

'I'm willing to get wet up to my ankles, if need be,' I said recklessly to my mother, 'if that's what it takes.'

'Oh dear! Did you bring spare socks?'

'No. But it won't kill me to have wet feet for an hour.'

'Oh, Noreen . . .'

'It'll be worth it to get to that island.'

My mother did not seem convinced.

We sat on a low wall and ate our sandwiches, looking out to sea. A seal stuck its head out of the water, then flipped itself upside down so that its scalloped tail popped up for a moment. It was interested in the kayakers paddling their long red boats round the edge of Damsay and the Holm. Lime-green shocks of pale weed stood out in pools against the khaki bladderwrack.

'I find that my little AeroPress,' my mother said abruptly, out of nowhere, 'is absolutely . . . all right.'

In the front seat of a parked car, a collie had twisted its head round to look at us hopefully.

We made our way back towards the beach. 'The tide'll be out by now,' I said, striding ahead, excited.

'It might be,' said my mother.

'It *will.*'

And as the road unspooled in front of us, there it was: the causeway. I whooped and raised my arms in the air.

'What is your plan once you get there?' my mother asked. 'Go up to the house—ask permission—and then . . .'

'Look around. Just sit with it.'

'We'll need to be quick. The tides can come back in very fast.'

'Half an hour or so. Not more,' I said soothingly.

I strode ahead onto the beach, and waited for my mother to catch up. 'Please absolutely don't go farther than you feel happy about,' I emphasized. 'I'm absolutely fine to go alone.'

'That's fine,' my mother said reservedly. 'I'm not sure you'll get as much as half an hour on the island, you know. Really. It would be terrible to get cut off.'

'Ten minutes,' I bargained, already making my way towards the Holm of Grimbister.

The stones on each side of the track were dry. Things had changed very fast: half an hour ago they'd been submerged in the axe-cold sea. Bladderwrack covered both sides of the causeway, but you could avoid it as you picked your way along the sharp mass of stones: there were two clear tracks, made perhaps by a tractor's wheels as it rolled towards the island. Every so often I glanced back at my mother. She was navigating slowly but surely, staring down at the ground.

Towards the end of the causeway was a rusted gate, which didn't seem to open on either side. It was part of a fence which rose up out of the sea on one side, and down back into it on the other, the fence posts surfacing to march sternly over the dry stones without looking at me. How did the people up at the house get in at all? I levered myself up onto the gate, stifling an exclamation when the bottom rail swung up under me, the whole gate tilting to sixty degrees. With a wobble and a bang, I got over, and waited for my mother. I held the gate steady with my whole weight against it as she pulled herself up.

'Oh,' my mother said, teetering. 'Oh.'

At the top she froze. But slowly we managed to talk her left boot up over the gate and onto the other side.

'What a fuss,' my mother said, half to herself, as she balanced with both feet on the bar.

'Some fusses are worth it,' I said, as she hopped down. She didn't respond.

But we were on the island now. It rose slightly in the centre, it's true; towards the sides, though, it seemed as level as a digestive biscuit. I hurried up the shingle, looped myself under the wire fence and up towards the one house. Through the window I could see a camera on a tripod but no signs of people.

'I don't think there's anyone in there,' I said, but my mother didn't hear me. There were sheep to the right and left; a fence, tied tightly shut with plastic twine, led to a field beyond, full of black cows looking at me. An oystercatcher wheeled overhead, letting out long, alarmed cheeps.

I leaned on the fence and gazed over the green grass at the sheep, clustering near the sea edge. They had left white and dark tufts, of wool and of shit, everywhere in the field. Overhead the clouds, blue

as a cat, swept in lines and thick ridges, and a wind turbine flapped
furiously. That was all. Beyond the field was the sea, and beyond the
sea the land, again.

I looked right round, sweeping my eye along the water which
enclosed this small piece of flat land. Holding it apart from the
mainland. Keeping it safe. I could see the island's edges, crisp and clear.

My mother had caught up with me. Without looking at her, I
said, 'Just give me another sixty seconds.'

'Of course. That's fine.'

The grass littered with itself. The broad flat round of the island.
The sound of the wind.

The clouds collapsed to grey fistfuls against a blazing pale sky.

I turned round and started to make my way back to the causeway.

But on the beach, I paused. While we'd been on the island, the tide
had gone down even farther, revealing a broadening collar of shingle,
expanding the circumference of the island. I started walking right,
away from the causeway, heading along the beach, and my mother
didn't stop me. And I was running now. I ran over the shingle, on this
tiny flat island which I'd chosen to be mine, over bladderwrack and
green slime. I dropped to one knee to pick up some whelk eggs, tossed
them back down, went on running. At the end of the beach was a small
standing stone with a narrow edge, barely reaching my waist, stained
with yellow lichen. I grabbed it hard and held it, in both hands, till
they hurt. It was a hug, a worship, a release. And then I turned round
and made my way back to where my mother stood waiting for me.

I looked back as we crept towards the mainland again, taking
our time, over the seaweed warty with bladders and barnacles. A
flat world off which one might fall. As we rode home on the bus,
peering out of the window, I could see that the sea hadn't yet taken
back the causeway.

The thing I'd found so hard about my cat Morvern's illness is that she hadn't told me anything about it. I realize how this sounds.

But Morvern had gone about her days quite normally, eating enthusiastically, twining round me, flinging herself on the ground and rolling. At no point had she let on that something was wrong. I'd felt so connected to her, and all that time she was seriously ill, and I didn't know. This is very normal for cats with kidney disease. They hide it until it's too severe to hide any longer. Cats live in solitude; there's no advantage to them in showing pain, as there might be for an animal which could expect help and care from the rest of its pack. For lone hunters, there are only disadvantages, because a sick animal is easy prey. I couldn't be angry or hurt by the deception: it was in her nature, as it was in mine. If I hoped my friends would understand when I vanished, it was only reasonable to try and understand when she did the same.

Our minds were inscrutable to each other. We could only ever make a guess at how the other one thought, felt, understood their world.

It didn't change anything about the fact that we loved each other.

And in realizing this, a small string knot untugged itself in my chest. It wouldn't stay untied: it would coil up again and again. But I'd got hold of an end now, and could pull it, sometimes, when I needed to.

'Look,' my mother said, on the last day in Orkney. We were coming off a beach at Stromness. I turned, and she was pointing down at something I'd missed: a spray of bones on a tuft of greened sand. 'I think that's a wing bone.'

'And a vertebra.' I picked it out of its grassy bedding and showed her.

'Ooh. Yes. And another one. There's the clavicle. Is that another wing?'

Crouched together, using our fingertips, my mother and I sorted through the bones.

The Way Home

تُوں کیہ باغے دی مولی حسینا

What worth are your small sufferings, Shah Hussain?

—Sanam Marvi, 'یار ویکھو'

The words for goodbye have changed since I left Pakistan. You used to say *khuda hafez*. Now it's *allah hafez*. What's changed is the name of God. The Persian word to the Arabic; a capacious, nonspecific word for God to a rigidly Muslim one.

In the early days of my banishment from Pakistan, shivering at school in Scotland in too-short black trousers which crackled with static, I learned that the town bookshop could order in any book you wanted, if you asked. So I did ask, eventually, for a book I'd wanted for years: *The Rebel's Silhouette*, a collection of poems by the Pakistani poet Faiz Ahmed Faiz, translated from Urdu by Agha Shahid Ali. I'd found a few of Ali's translations online in Pakistan, and was hooked. I printed my favourites out, and stuck bands of Sellotape across them to protect them from water damage, and tied them together into a little booklet with string, to carry around with me and pull out when the beat of the half-remembered lines in my head grew too strong to ignore. In Britain, though, you didn't need to resort to DIY. Shops would sell you almost anything you could think of, and I upgraded to the whole collection. The Urdu font on the left-hand pages was stylized and difficult, but I flicked back and forth between the original and Ali's translations, and very slowly I made out most of the meaning. The meaning which Ali caught and shaped into English, and the meanings that slipped through translation, telling a different story, on the opposite page.

One poem lit up the spaces in my head.

> *On each patch of green, from one shade to the next,*
> *the noon is erasing itself by wiping out all color,*
>
> *. . .*
>
> *In the distance,*
> *there are terrible sorrows, like tides . . .*
> *They've turned the horizon to mist.*
> *And behind that mist is the city of lights,*
> *my city of many lights.*

I could see the white-grey sky of a winter day in Lahore: cold mist mixing itself into smog, the patchy green stubble along the wire fences. I could smell that chill bitter air.

> *How will I return to you, my city,*
> *where is the road to your lights?*

Underneath the Urdu poem, I could read what was missing from the English translation: *Lahore Jail, 28 March; Montgomery Jail, 15 April 1954.* Faiz, a Communist, was imprisoned for four years in Pakistan for alleged conspiracy against the government. In prison, he wrote poetry. So perhaps for him—held apart by jail walls—the city of many lights was Lahore. It certainly was for me. When the plane had lifted me into the sky above Pakistan for the last time, carrying us away, I'd pressed my face against the window trying to burn the pattern of yellow lights below onto my eyes, so that when I closed them again I'd be able to see Lahore, forever. *Oh city, my city of many lights.*

The flat fields in Lahore, upon which my life stands, have vanished. I have spent years searching for them. I cannot go back to find them in person. Going to Pakistan at all would be complicated and unsafe. To renew my expired Pakistani passport, I need a signature from either a father or a husband. Even if I skirt that—husbandless, fatherless—I'm down as Muslim in my records, and so I'd need to sign a declaration testifying to my belief that Muhammad was the very last prophet, and that anyone believing otherwise isn't a Muslim. This is a jab against the Ahmadi Muslims: one of the most persecuted minorities in Pakistan, subject to state-sponsored hate, because they believe in another prophet after Muhammad. Pakistan barely recognizes or acknowledges its first Nobel Prize winner, Abdus Salam, because he is Ahmadi. What a way to begin a journey back to a place where I lived in fear and secrecy: to lie, and to take part in an act of hate.

And if I were to return to Pakistan—where would I stay? I haven't spoken to my Pakistani family in years, except a few words to my shell-shocked cousin, the morning after my father's death: he could only repeat the same phrase in English, over and over again, no matter what I asked him. I wouldn't be able to go back to Lahore without the whisper network sending the news flaming to my family. And if I stayed in a hotel, how could I move around safely, with my rusty, never-fluent Urdu?

And what could I say to a rickshaw driver? 'Take me to some fields, if they're still here.'

And even if I found the fields: What would they mean?

What old bones would I find there, and what would I do with them?

The last time I saw my father, we met at Liverpool Street Station in 2012. It was eleven years since he'd dismissed my youngest sister Forget-Me-Not's first seizure as a migraine, and seven years since he banished my eldest sister Rabbit for being framed in a photograph. He had come to the UK for work and—while he was there—to visit Forget-Me-Not, the only child he hadn't disowned.

('She still loves me,' he'd said the day he'd disowned the rest of us, clutching her as we watched. My little sister stared and shook.)

In her obedience, Forget-Me-Not travelled down alone from my grandmother's house in Scotland, to meet him in London. She'd passed on a request from him to me, to join them there. I'd responded to him tersely: Why do you want to meet me?

> Why do I want to see you? [my father wrote back] Well I would, certainly, not like to dwell on the past and instead would like to build a few bridges. To have fun together and make a few happy memories for all of us.

I refused to get involved. I had enough on my plate. I was groping along in Cambridge, trying to eat and to not die and to finish my master's degree. But three days into the visit, Forget-Me-Not phoned me in tears.

'He's saying things I don't understand,' she sobbed. 'Things about you and the others. I don't understand. Please come. Please come.'

And in the end I came, because I was still strapped to her, crushed against her in the back seat of the car, forever.

As I approached the ticket barriers, I saw Forget-Me-Not waiting on the other side, swaddled in far too many clothes, as usual, and my father beside her, dressed as exquisitely as a doll in charcoal-grey, with red flowers in his hands. They were standing very carefully together.

I hadn't seen my father for seven years, but my stiffening body hadn't forgotten. It pulled my eyes straight to his angular face, his white hair and glasses, incongruous against the English signs and grey morning light. The most unsettling and most natural thing: as though part of me had been waiting all this time to see him again.

I had time to prepare my face as I approached. Too much time. I managed to assemble a fixed, confident expression, but it shivered into a strain by the time I reached them.

My sister's face showed pure relief. My father handed me the flowers and pulled me, without permission, into a hug. I knew, then, that I'd lost. The situation had been so thoroughly pre-empted that all I could do was cooperate. From that point on, I froze.

But we weren't supposed to dwell on the past. All that was water under the bridges that we were meant to be building. Meanwhile, Forget-Me-Not was wrapped up in layers, to keep her safe from the chills which might trigger a seizure, and I was wearing a brown leather jacket over a short floral dress, because it was the closest I could get to *fuck you*.

'What are you studying at Cambridge?' he asked, over orange juice in the hotel lobby.

'English,' I said, and watched the shiver of disgust pass over his face.

'And what then? What will you do after that?'

'I'll teach at a university,' I said, and smiled blandly. This was a confidence I didn't feel. Cambridge had funded my master's degree, which had won me another year of a life, another small space to edge my feet out into. But it ended in June. I fully expected to be dead in a caravan that time the following year, my body beginning to shrivel and smell. That was my plan. I'd buy a static caravan with my savings, and put it in an empty field somewhere, and hide there till I died.

But, for the moment, it was still only March. And in London my father contemplated my answer for a moment, then smiled and nodded. 'Yes. That's okay.'

I was livid. He still thought his approval mattered to me. He still thought he got the sign-off on my decisions.

But I wasn't here to fight. I was here to place myself, as solidly as possible, between him and Forget-Me-Not. I felt myself going stony and faraway again.

As we walked through London, I told jokes, and drew Forget-Me-Not into the chat, and met my father's gaze with empty, practised ease. I made myself disappear, turned myself into a space that could hold whatever happened. There's a photograph from that day that my father took, which I can't bear to look at: Forget-Me-Not and me, against the artful stone walls of an Italian restaurant, my arm round her shoulders as instructed. My father had insisted on buying us expensive, ridiculous red soft drinks, with sprigs of mint and two straws each. We're smiling, but there are sacks under her eyes, and I'm glancing out at him like an explosive.

The strain grew unbearable. It was a relief when we gave up, and—as though we'd agreed aloud—made our way to their hotel room, wordlessly, and my father and I sat facing each other in chairs by the window. I put my feet up on the windowsill, stretching out my obscene bare legs in their sandals, and smiled at him as though daring him to comment.

'I know you think I am a monster,' he said. 'But try to understand. You were brainwashed. Your mother brainwashed you into hating me.'

Forget-Me-Not sat on one of the twin beds. 'Please. Can we not fight.'

'We're not fighting,' I said.

Forget-Me-Not wasn't convinced. She cried, first quietly, then loudly, her eyes sparking and her eyelids trembling. I ignored her.

'I know you don't like me,' I said.

The flat truth stretched between us. We could both see it. It was what we had in common.

Forget-Me-Not lay down. Her limbs were starting to twitch and discolour. 'Please,' she chanted. 'Please stop, please stop, please stop.'

'We have to talk about these things,' I said, with one eye still on my father.

'This is just a conversation,' my father said imploringly. 'Just talking. We are not fighting. It's just that in life, everyone sees things differently. Look. You see, life is like—' He cast around, then snatched a mug up from the tea station. 'Like this cup.'

I cringed.

'I hold it like this, between my hands. You see the handle. I do not. There are two perspectives. Which one is true? Who can say?'

My father held the mug beseechingly up to his youngest daughter, who was long past seeing or understanding anything at this point. Her eyes had filmed and started to roll back in her head. How absurd he was, I thought, standing by the window. How absurd and self-important. And tiny, in his charcoal suit, trying to take charge of language. Holding up a cheap metaphor to a young, disabled person as she started to seize.

'We need to stop,' I said, with effort. I didn't want to stop. I wanted to win this fight that we weren't having. 'We all need to calm down. Forget-Me-Not's going to have a fit.'

'A fit?' My father peered down at my sister, whose mottled limbs were splayed among the mussed sheets and blankets.

'We need to stop talking about this,' I said. 'Let's go outside. Have dinner, maybe. Are you hungry, Forget-Me-Not?'

I took the mug from him and put it down.

The next thing I remember is the three of us sitting in an Indian restaurant. My father made a big thing of ordering off-menu, demanding complicated dishes which involved running out for extra ingredients, speaking to the staff in Urdu. They gave him tolerant, embarrassed looks, politely half disguising the fact that they didn't think him special, and after a respectful pause they brought out the same yellow meals they served to all their clientele.

Rebuffed, my father watched me as I made myself eat.

'Don't eat naan like that,' he said. I'd always pulled off pieces of crust and split them with both hands—instead of using just my right hand, as was correct—before using the butterflied shell to scoop up food. 'This is how you eat with naan.'

I would not look at his hands. 'This is how I eat with naan,' I said. I was twenty-two. It was too late to teach me how to eat.

'I was always frightened to touch you,' he said later, when the remains of the rice had gone cold and the *salan* was yellow smears on our plates. 'You were always so cold. Even when you were a tiny baby. You had a cold look in your eyes.'

He laughed, like a puff or a choke, and reached out very awkwardly to touch the hair by my ear. I watched his hand as it approached. This is the only part I remember vividly. The way my breath caught in my body. His fingertips brushed the loose curl, then dropped.

Afterwards, he saw me off at the station barriers, back to Cambridge. We never spoke again. My little sister told me later: 'He said you were dishonest.'

This was true. But the only honest thing would have been not to come at all.

And then, eight years later, he died.

Five years after I saw my father for the last time, my friend Rima came to visit me in Oxford, and Pakistan bloomed suddenly into my life again.

Rima joined my school in Lahore when I was fifteen. She came to class on the first day with purple tips in her hair, and everyone sat up and paid attention. She wrote poems on a typewriter that her father had bought her, when he saw how much she loved literature. He understood that the aesthetics of how we make poems might also matter to her: the smell of typewriter ink, the flexing ribbon, the clack of keys. In a sense, it was an absurd purchase. But he gave her a typewriter because he loved who she was.

I was known, also, to like poetry. At fifteen I was very thin, and so were my eyebrows, from pulling, and the bloodied bald spot on top of my head was growing all the time, as things at home got worse. But I'd commandeered a small whiteboard from somewhere, and propped it up in the corner of the classroom. Every day I would find and learn a small poem on the internet, and write it up on the board the next day. If God had died inside me, I needed something else there instead. For me, at that point, it was poetry.

So Rima and I became friends, and after a short time she started bringing me her poems, typed on lined paper and folded over, sometimes with a flower tucked inside, to read and respond to. I couldn't do much, but I knew I could treat them as though they mattered. I read them with her and told her which bits I liked. And I kept them all, in a buckled black ring binder that Spot had discarded. When I left Lahore a year later, I gave them all back to her, filed in that folder. She turned over the pages, stunned. They had transformed into something new in my custody: an archive.

When she grew up, Rima moved to Delft, and published those poems in a book, and at some point she acquired a hijab, a husband and a child. I was living on my own in Oxford, struggling through the last bumpy months of a doctorate. But when Rima arrived at my room in Oxford, her big, deep-lidded eyes were the same, and when she tickled my nose—emerging lopsided as ever from my face, like a huge tooth—and called it 'Bumpy,' as she always had, I felt fifteen and foolish once more.

I couldn't stop looking at Rima, reassuring myself that she really was here, incongruously, in the middle of my daily British life. But also, I couldn't really meet her eye. I'd vanished so suddenly from Lahore, without an explanation, my school uniform hanging off me in folds. I took her round Oxford, and showed her the college where I worked. She sat under a tree in the manicured garden, reserved for an exclusive, privileged few, and laughed at me. 'This is so weird. In the Netherlands, there isn't this sort of university hierarchy. All the universities are considered equally good. I don't see the point of this exclusion.' And she was right, of course. We talked about her PhD and mine, about her son's love of purple flowers. He was four, and touched small things in the garden very gently; living between Urdu and English and Dutch, he was quiet, in these early years, as he sorted through language. So we watched as he lifted plants in the cup of his hands, and collected pine cones, arranging them into shapes.

Rima wore her new hijab wrapped around her hair, leaving her neck clear: a style I'd never seen in Pakistan. It looked beautiful. She brought the subject up herself, without prompting.

'It was when I was in Malaysia that I started. These women asked me: Do you want to come to mosque with us? And I was just . . . amazed, Noreen. I told them: in Pakistan women don't go to mosque, that's only for men. And they were so surprised. It's like a completely different version of Islam over there, it's much more equal for men and women. And no one forces you. Being there and meeting those girls made me want to wear hijab. To feel closer to my God.'

'What did your family say?'

'Oh, they were *not* happy! You know, in Lahore it looks bad, they think it makes the family look backward. My dad talked to me for hours on the phone, trying to persuade me to take it off. But now they just accept it. They understand that it's my business.'

Later, we sat cross-legged on my bed and ate pizza out of the box as night fell over west Oxford.

'Do you remember mango bugs?'

'Is that what they were called? God, they were the worst! Like white pills, all over the trees!'

'And when you stood on them, they popped, and they were nothing but green goo.'

We were starting to relax. Rima moved to lie down, and she was smiling up at me. Her little son flung himself bodily over her, and grinned at us both.

'You used to like the French fries from the tuck shop. I remember. Even when Zainab put so much chilli powder on them your eyes watered.'

'And kissing your Islamiat book if you dropped it in the dust!'

'No one knows these things, do they? You only know if you were there.'

We were quiet for a minute. I lay down next to her on the bed and closed my eyes.

'I'm sorry I didn't say I was going,' I said eventually. 'We only had a week to pack everything. And he—my dad—made us promise not to tell anyone.'

'I know,' Rima said. 'I know.'

'I wanted to tell you. It was so awful.'

'I knew the girl who did it, did I tell you? Who sent the photographs to him. Spiteful. No one else would have said anything. That kind of girl is always trying to get attention.'

We breathed together.

'We all know now,' said Rima. 'Don't worry.'

I heard a sliding rustle as Rima closed the pizza box. She was satisfied. But she didn't know what I wanted her to know. I wanted to give her the key to everything that had happened, and to who I was. I'd never dared tell anyone before. But I hoped she would recognize it.

'I remember something else from Pakistan, you know.' My voice was thick. 'I wonder if you know it too. There were these fields. Really big ones, near Model Town. Totally empty and flat. With a blue sign on them, saying they were going to build a hospital there.'

Rima was silent.

'Did you know those fields?' I pressed.

'I . . . can't think of any big fields,' Rima said. 'Were they outside the city?'

'No. Near Model Town. You turned a corner, and suddenly there they were. Near Model Town,' I repeated, stupidly. 'Really big.'

Why couldn't I remember anything? Why couldn't I locate myself in a place I'd lived more than half my life?

'Okay,' Rima said. I could feel her incomprehension and—worse—her kindness, in her long pause; she was thinking about how to handle this latest eccentric tangent. My preoccupations which I couldn't make reasonable or legible. And I burned. 'They've probably been built over now. Land in Lahore has become so expensive. I can't imagine any place being left empty.'

'Probably,' I agreed, and something small in me sank and died, and I opened my eyes and smiled and took another slice of pizza.

Four years later, in a final search for those fields, I typed my childhood address into Google Maps, and Google Maps came up shrugging. It could find the right district in Lahore and the right block of streets. But when I zoomed in, all the roads were numbered in a way I'd never seen before. Obviously some sort of reshuffle had taken place: a periodic rationalization of how things were organized. The house code I had searched for no longer existed. Other things had changed too. When I was growing up, Pakistan's fourth province still bore its clinical British name: North-West Frontier Province. Now it was Khyber Pakhtunkhwa. I went to Wikipedia, found the name in Urdu, and sounded it out carefully to work out how to pronounce it.

With words failing to connect me—to help me find my home or let go of it—I switched to satellite view and studied the scene. A graveyard caught my eye, a large wedge of green in the next block over. My father, I'd gathered, had been buried in a local graveyard; I didn't know any more than that. Maybe this was where his body was, now. Or the clay where his body had been.

There was also a park, but its shape from the air meant nothing to me. I couldn't translate it into my memories of the parks we visited and gave our own names to: Peacock Park, Linear Park. I remembered the main road, Akbar Chowk, but the monument that marked it when we lived there—a peach-coloured stylization of God's finger curving round and pointing up to Heaven—seemed to have been levelled. Around the space, new traders and shops had bloomed, like daisies, their names meaning nothing to me. *Education Academy. Sweet-O! Fri Chicks. Decent Boys Hostel.*

And Google's magnification stopped well above the level of individual houses. Presumably they had decided this was close enough for a country like Pakistan; close enough to satisfy the extent of anyone's curiosity about a place like this. When I zoomed in further, there were only blurs of white and beige pixels, vaguely approximating the flat roofs of my childhood. Bigger patches of beige might be larger houses. Or they might be empty lots, like the one which used to sit opposite my home, filling with goats when a herd came through, and suddenly emptying again. There was no way of knowing. I couldn't find my way back.

I zoomed back out, still searching for those huge, aching fields. I didn't even know which direction to look in, on this inscrutable bird's-eye view of a place I was only ever lost beneath, inside. I looked and looked, but nothing offered itself. There were possibilities: a sports ground, near a hospital, by a plant nursery. That might line up. But the sites I found were brown, mostly, with only speckles of green. And they looked so small on the map. Little postage stamps, posted into a child's tiny life, years before.

A flat landscape stretches out blandly. It says nothing, and it hides nothing. It takes everything that's happened on it and to it and smooths it out till there's nothing to see. Nothing to love, either, none of the rises and falls which signify feeling and life. It's not a place people can empathize with. It's not a good victim. Its suffering doesn't seem to matter. Easy to read it as empty, something waiting passively to be exploited—in fact, something made to be exploited: built on, used, farmed, eliminated. So we heap more on it, more and more. Or we leave it to be waste.

Landscapes are the sites of so much pain, and flatlands are no exception; pain's been compacted and trodden into them over hundreds of years. In North America, the endless prairie beckoned white settlers towards a spare, unspooling horizon. Culturally specific ideas of 'efficiency' and 'waste avoidance' led them to colonize and build on those prairies, whether rich and fertile or hard, with sod needing to be coaxed out of the earth. But, of course, these lands were not empty, convenient as it was to think of them that way. Pretending that they were was an act of violence against the indigenous people who lived there. Who still live there, whether or not it is convenient for the West to admit it.

The flat lands I have loved also contain the stretched pain of people of colour forced into difficult, dangerous work by border regimes, or omitted from histories where their presence is an inconvenience. The human zoo on Newcastle Town Moor, quietly buried in the archives. The cockle pickers who died on Morecambe Bay. The seawall built by Chinese migrants, who laboured and endured and risked themselves for our war, only to be written out of it. But Britain prefers not to know quite what goes on in its flat places. When it turns its eye there, all there is to see is the wet sky and the sand, and the wind rattling in the leaves of the shrivelled waymarkers.

How, and what, do we know? A flat landscape tells me that we can never really know ourselves, let alone anyone or anything *other*. And so it gives me an ethics to live by. We think we need to empathize—to feel another person's feelings—in order to relate to them and care for them. But we can never penetrate into others, feel what they feel, see what they see.

All we can do is to believe what people tell us. Even—perhaps especially—when we can't ourselves understand it.

My life in Pakistan—I think now—was like a bare field, with nothing to strive towards or hope for, and a wind blowing hard, straight across that flat space. My years in Pakistan will haunt me all my life. I move my mind over its stretches, in small circles and in large ones.

But Pakistan isn't the flat place.

One is often misread. One is especially often misread if one is a woman of colour. So: the flat place is not Pakistan. Pakistan is not the place of trauma, of lack, of pain.

The flat place is what happens when one's reality is at odds with that of everyone else. When one's truth comes starkly into contact with a world which denies it. Which cannot see it.

Pakistan was the real part of my life. When I boil my life right down, what crystallizes round the edges and flakes off is Pakistan. That was where the things happened which British people don't want to think about. The gardener who was tortured by the police, big blocks of wood dug into his calf muscles at the corners till he screamed. The children picking through the rubbish heaps. Children with polio. Children with missing limbs. Children with burns over half their faces, leaving one wide, forever-open eye. Children who were much, much worse off than I was, than I would ever be.

This violent, hateful world is as real in Britain as it is in Pakistan. It happens in Britain, right now, as well as in the places Britain left in pieces when it had finished playing out its imperial fantasies. But Britain still won't let itself know that.

When it was an empire, Britain shipped its shit abroad to its colonies, in a very literal sense. It forcibly exported its cheap, crude cotton fabric to India, for instance, destroying South Asian industries for English profit. (In fact, it still sends its rubbish abroad—its tainted recycling, its piles of landfill—to become the problem of other countries, which don't contain white people and which therefore seem to matter less.) But also: it exported its psychological shit. Its hang-ups, its hatreds, its moral panics. It was under the British Raj that homosexuality was codified as a criminal offence. Now Britain, supposedly progressive, looks back at homophobia in its ex-colonies and tuts disapprovingly.

In fact, the very existence of Pakistan—riven by religious anxiety, intolerance and rigidity—derived from the philosophies that empire brought with it. Britain's 'divide and rule' policy whipped up tensions between Hindus and Muslims, until it seemed to some that the only way for Muslims in the subcontinent to survive was to have their own state. The Raj, effectively, imagined the country, and its central premise, into existence, until Pakistan ejected itself by force from the empire in pain and crisis.

And then, when Cyril Radcliffe had drawn his sloppy line down the subcontinent in 1947—and when the fallout from this division was violence, rape and murder—Britain refused to hear it. Mountbatten, the last British viceroy of India, defended the death toll prudishly in 1962 as 'not more than 250,000 dead.' It could have been anything up to five million. We don't know, precisely because Britain couldn't be bothered to know; it was too busy hoisting itself out of the country, after almost a hundred years of direct rule, preoccupied with world wars which had turned out more expensive than planned.

The West makes a strange demand of the East: that non-white people should somehow be untraumatized by things which would leave a white person reeling. That because those things are 'normal there'—a horrifying normal, in this case, grown out of a bungled withdrawal from a violent empire—they somehow leave no impact on the people who go through them. Like my grandmother, who endured Partition. Like my father, who at seventeen fought in a civil war. They never talked about either experience.

Why would you speak if you don't trust anyone to listen or care?

Britain sent its shit to Pakistan. And in Pakistan, it settled and stayed. Lahore had no waste-disposal system. There are no drains in the roads. But at least you could see it. Nothing was hidden: not the rubbish, not the electricity pylons which barred the city skies.

When I came to Britain, Pakistan was still real. It was still the real thing. It was just that no one around me could see it. The things I'd seen and lived through were still going on, worse and worse, and in Britain too: poverty and racism and sexism. I arrived in Britain in 2005. Raunch culture was at its height; I was stunned to see Playboy bunnies printed on children's pencil cases in the shops. No one seemed to notice how bad things were for women in this supposedly liberated country. In Pakistan, we talked about women's rights, called ourselves feminists. Here, the response was a shrug: Feminism was over, right? The bad things were right there in front of me, and no one was talking about them. On the TV, in *Little Britain*, David Walliams blacked up, and everybody laughed. On the streets, homeless people hunched on the pavements, and British people strode by as though this were normal, in one of the wealthiest of all countries.

Now, living in the UK, I do know that the world around me is real too. That Britain—with clean water coming straight out of the taps, and people laughing in the pub after work, and fish fingers in the freezer and advertisements on the TV—is real. But Pakistan stored a wordless knowledge inside me—a sure, horrifying, beautiful certainty—which is wholly at odds with the world I now live in: a reality that Britain can't absorb.

And I don't want to stop feeling the way I do. I don't want to give up knowing, in this very visceral way, what I know about people and what they can do to you. About countries and what they can do to you. I don't want ever to be wholly relaxed, wholly at home, in a world of flowing fresh water built on the parched pain of others. The world itches, and so it should.

When there is a truth which affirms itself insistently in a way that has no end and no resolution, when it receives no responsiveness or recognition, and has nowhere to site itself but in itself, entrenched in its own starkness—that's the flat place.

Cassandra, screaming, was in the flat place.

Or rather, she entered it when the screaming, finally, stopped.

During the summer of 2020, the Black Lives Matter movement gained steam rapidly across the West, spreading out from the United States, where the state-sponsored murder of George Floyd had ignited public outrage. And in the aftermath of this wave of protest and dissent, new attention was turned on Britain's social norms; opened up like figs, their racism was laid bare.

Suddenly the things which I had, unconsciously, decided to tolerate were revealed as *intolerable*. It was legitimately inhumane to make oneself tolerate these things: that was what was revealed to me. One could demand better ways of being represented, without bargaining, without caricature. Suddenly there were people of colour speaking up, saying things I'd barely let myself think, demands I'd never even dreamed of making—and, in total, all these demands added up to being treated like a human being.

Areas of overlap were beginning to emerge, to be acknowledged, between my reality and those of other people. And I noticed that the flat place inside me didn't vanish, or even really fade, during these moments of shared reality, or of expressing my own reality and seeing it accepted by those around me. But something about it warmed. It drew in—I can't explain—towards the heart of itself, like a string bag being drawn shut. And the colours of its landscape saturated, into purples and yellows and rosy oranges. I would always live in the flatland. But that might be all right. Because from time to time the wind stopped howling across it, leaving only the particular quiet of spring warmth, against a grey sky, as flowers began to put their minds to uncurling. And I could stop looking at the sky, and simply trace my fingers through the loose soil on the surface.

I don't expect to set foot in Pakistan ever again. In some situations, there is no possibility of a healing return, a reconciliation. My father is dead; my mother has established the mental territory through which she is willing to move. My sisters and I find it very difficult to be near one another. The small devices we've built, each on our own, to help us survive, out of tinfoil and cardboard and cheap tape, fall apart when we gather; a centripetal force drives us back and down into the back seat of my uncle's car, which will always be waiting for us, even now.

All families are cults. All parents let their children down.

When I think about my father, two truths sit side by side. On one hand: the knowledge that he chose to transcend all the pressures of culture and masculinity which pressed in on him at every side, telling him that girls couldn't be boys, girls weren't worth educating.

On the other hand: the knowledge that if our childhood was a vast, failed experiment in resisting these cultural strictures, then we became lab rats to him.

My father did it, in the end, because he could, because there was no one to stop him. No one to even raise an eyebrow. No one around him thought it was wrong or blamed him. In such a situation, in the face of fatigue or distraction or impatience, which of us would have gone out of our way to do better? We are kept only very thinly, by laws or reproaches or disapproving looks, from doing terrible things. When society lets us get away with it, we will do them.

I think people only act as best they can. And that goes for me too. I don't blame him. But I don't forgive him either.

A few years ago, I found a photograph on Facebook of his funeral: My father in his white shroud. His face wider and stiffer than I remember, eyes closed, two purple spots on his lower lip where they must have tried to intubate him. Red rose petals scattered around his head, and a hand reaching out from off-screen to pull a dark green velvet cover over his face. I keep that photograph saved on my computer, and I look at it whenever I need to remember that he truly is dead. He doesn't matter any more. He's just bones in the ground now, and he can stay there. My own bones, full of holes, are dragging themselves on.

Some things stay unresolved. You make peace with their active, living presence in your life. You live in, and with, the charged absence. And perhaps that can be a good thing. Perhaps—at its best—living with the doubt and uncertainty can open a person up to possibility, can help you to shrug off the ego that needs to control and to dominate. Knowing that it can be meaningful to focus on the 'wrong' details. To make strange relationships with strange things. To allow a scene to blur out of vision, generously. At its best, that's how the flat place feels to me. It doesn't steer you or demand that you move in a particular direction. If it's a place of terror and despair, pressed right up against the cold ground of something true, it's also—and precisely because of that—a place where new kinds of connection might start, very furtively, to grow. That's what's terrifying and wonderful about it.

Donald Winnicott thought that living a good life after trauma means being able to be safely and absorbedly inside yourself. Not spending your time alert to what is going on outside: hearing the distant screams, smelling the burning. It means being able to simply *be*, rather than always responding to things in your environment.

But I wonder whether this is a kind of deliberate ignorance. People think of flatness as numb and dead. But the flat place means being alive to things which are plausibly deniable, which happened just faintly or incidentally enough that most people feel able to ignore them. Allowing myself just to *be* has often felt like an inexcusable withdrawing from responsibility.

'I worry,' I said to my therapist, when things were starting at last to look a little brighter, 'I worry that when I'm better—when I'm able to connect in a way that's nourishing to me, when I don't have to notice everything, when I don't go numb in these weird ways or make people turn into pot plants to cope with them—that I'll have lost something. The thing that I like about myself. That makes my mind work differently, that brings some kind of originality to my work. I'm scared I'll lose that.'

And for once, my therapist looked very serious indeed.

'Once you've known what it is to think and feel what you've had to think and feel,' she said, 'once you've been where you are, and been shaped as you have by your life—when the very first experiences you've had made you a certain way—you don't need to worry that this way of seeing will go. It will always be there, in you, even if other ways of seeing and connecting become more instinctive to you. You will never lose it.'

It could have sounded so sad, so defeatist, in any other context. But that made me feel better about trying to feel better. Knowing that one foot would always be able to drop right down, like a swimmer in the deep end, and touch the floor of the flat place. The skin of another reality, one which I could revisit when I needed to, even if it stopped feeling like the only surface of the real.

You can spend your whole life trying to remember. Digging around painfully, like tweezers searching for an ingrown hair, till the blood starts.

We're frightened of forgetting. We talk about how to stop it. Can we delay cognitive decline? Can we bring back lost memories? People are fascinated by the idea that nothing is ever forgotten, only repressed or mislaid in our capacious but badly filed brains. As though hoarding memory will keep us intact: a continuous tightrope on which we can edge through our lives. As though memory were not always pouring off both sides, all the time, at every moment.

I can't hold up what I remember as any kind of explanation. My memories matter to me. But they cannot matter to you. When you face me, I offer up something onto which—I think—you might grasp. But—like the low trees of the fens, the flowers in the hedges—it's not enough. You pause on it, stymied, then pass on.

To come to terms with myself—my ambiguously damaged self—I must become okay with that form of contact, of touch. To feel that I don't need to explain that surface which defies attention or comprehension. I started out by thinking I needed to learn to make the leap of faith; to take the risk of putting my world into words, offering up to others what lay inside me. And I think this is right. This is what I am doing. But there's another leap that I am starting to be able to make: to make the offering without explanation, and not to mind if sometimes I receive blank looks in return. Countless tiny things, which I cannot make mean anything in themselves, have compacted into the firm peat of my life, the surface over which I walk. What matters now is that surface. I stand on it all the time. It's always with me.

Some time before my trip to Suffolk, the first journey I took in what would become the long process of writing this book, a friend tagged me on Twitter. 'This made me think of you,' he wrote, attaching a painting of windmills in the fens. 'I do love these landscapes, despite the damage that draining them has done.'

The fens are marked, and made distinctive, by their damage. Drainage brought flat, arable, farmable land. It also stripped locals of a way of life, and massacred biodiversity. The landscape demands a strange double vision: rich with fertility and a symbol of death; smooth and perfect, and yet a place where something went very wrong. It's impossible to separate the two. Is the life marked by loss? Does the life spring forth from that loss?

It's pointless to try and decide which the 'real' fens are: the marshland alive with chirrups and splashes, or these drained farmlands. Because nature is damage. It's one thing damaging another, a fox killing a rabbit, mistletoe burrowing into a tree, dead things piling up and making peat. We think of ecology as a kind of harmony, but equilibrium is just as much about the balance of death as of life.

We can't live in this world without damaging or being damaged. The point is to be deliberate about which damage to give and take.

Complex trauma is a controversial and complicated diagnosis for a number of reasons. One reason people give for resisting the diagnosis—preferring alternatives or avoiding diagnosis at all— is that they feel it establishes their damage as irrevocable. That everything they do involves creeping through this twilight life, fundamentally and permanently marked.

On the one hand, I don't believe complex trauma is irrevocable. I think—I hope—that there are ways to throw thin new strings across that blasted mental landscape, to touch and connect and feel my way into shapes and sensations that would once have been unimaginable to me. Finding comfort in other people's presence, rather than breathing only once I'm out of their sight. Talking to people without derealizing them. I notice it getting better. I notice, now, when people suddenly slide into unreality for me, when they become pot plants or two-dimensional collections of pixels. Noticing is a sign that they were, briefly, real.

On the other hand, I think people are too frightened of the irrevocable. As though anything short of being able to restart the game from scratch is a catastrophe. But we must make a life inside the worlds that we find ourselves in. It's not for me to say whether or not I'm permanently broken. If the past has flattened me into something unsharable and burning—if I'm a damaged landscape, and I never rise into the peaks or fall into the troughs of desire, energy, response, connection that other people experience—then that's all right. Something new has been made. In this space, there's life.

In the memory, I'm four or five. I know because the figures bending over the stove and the countertop are too tall to be relevant. They don't have faces. Instead, I'm on a level with the kitchen cupboards. When you open them at night, they're dark and frightening; you see the glinting eyes of frogs at the back, among the pots. But it's mid-morning now, and lunch is being cooked. Silver pans are swilling onions and garlic and chillies juicily around their mouths, sucking and hissing. I'm heading towards the light of the veranda, where roti is rolled out and slapped from hand to hand and puffed over an open flame. I'm following a word. *Hai.* Meaning, in Urdu: 'is,' or 'to be.' You put it at the end of a sentence, when you are finished. *Hai.* 'It is.' Finished. Done. The word twists in my mind, turns sleek and brown, into its English homophone, 'hare.' I follow the hare through to the light. I can see it in front of me. It is finished.

Epilogue

'Are you ready?'

I shut my eyes. 'Yes.'

We're on my best friend's houseboat. It's dark outside, and inside, except for the glow of the fire and the fairy lights she's looped around the corners of the bunk. I'm lying on my side, with my back to her.

'Okay,' my best friend says. She laughs nervously and reaches a hand round my waist, before pulling it back on a reflex. This is so odd for her, I think quietly, staring at the wood panelling in front of my face. But she's apologizing already, and then, resolutely, both her arms circle around me, and her hands come to rest on my stomach.

'What do you want me to do?' she asks, and she sounds only a little bit frightened.

I think. Once I babysat a little girl who announced, when I put her to bed, that she wouldn't be able to sleep unless I stroked her tummy like her mummy and daddy did. Astounding, I thought, to be able to demand that so confidently. Petrified, rigid, I ran my hand gingerly over the child's belly, moving it about three inches each way from the centre, pretending to breathe, pretending this was normal, as she drifted off to sleep.

'Can you stroke it?' I ask. 'Maybe in circles. Small ones and big ones.'

My friend's hands are so nervous, twitching and hesitant, but I hardly notice. I'm focused on what my stomach is doing. It doesn't understand. It's so scared, and so excited. It leaps and jerks under her touch, cramps into pain and sags out into butter, testing this new situation. But I've warned my best friend that this might happen, and she keeps going.

After a while I bring my own hands up and put them over hers. With her, I cup the little handful of belly my body releases when I lie on my side. I press down, gently and firmly. I squeeze. I hold.

I pat my stomach gently, with her hand. 'It's okay,' I whisper, in the voice I keep for myself. 'It's okay.'

Then I take my hands away, and my best friend, one of the loves of my life, circles my stomach gently, tenderly, with her hands, and whispers *it's okay* in my ear. And there are a few moments when all of us—her, me, the boat, the fire, my stomach and her hands—are all together, real, in the same place, at the same time.

A Note: Words and Debts

This book did not begin its life as a narrative about complex post-traumatic stress disorder (cPTSD). It was, solely, a study of encounters with flat landscapes. It was in writing it, and in discussion with my agent, that I came to understand that the complex trauma I sustained in my early life was an element which could not be omitted.

Legitimate concern exists about 'trauma' as a distinctively Western paradigm; about the applicability of PTSD and its underlying assumptions to communities which privilege the collective self over the individual self; about PTSD's capacity to drown out or negate other kinds of responses to suffering; about PTSD diagnoses as a way of pathologizing sane responses to an insane world. I speak only for myself in this book, out of one (remarkable and precious) therapeutic relationship, which has only ever legitimized my anger about racial and economic injustice, rather than trying to anaesthetize it, and which seeks to support me to reenter the collective (whatever that may be) in my own ways and on survivable terms.

Everyone's experience is different. People diagnosed with cPTSD may not find themselves mirrored in this book. Other people without the diagnosis, or with a different diagnosis, might feel a kinship with what I describe. Complex PTSD is one of the terms that my therapist has used with me, alongside others, such as 'developmental trauma.' I am less interested in the diagnosis, or the term, than in the particularities of the way I experience my life, its brightness and its struggles. If the shorthand of cPTSD helps to make that tangible, I am happy.

In general, when talking to friends, I am more likely to talk about 'the effects of the life I've had' than 'my cPTSD.' This is a personal preference, because I do not experience my mental illness as something separable from me, like a pet that I carry around. I opened my eyes into it and have lived within it ever since. It is me.

But I use the term cPTSD here because I think it makes what I am talking about more legible. In this way, it can be Googled, described, made concrete. I use the term, even though it is not my favourite, because part of the work one has to do, I think, is to find a way to live—in the smallest, safest ways—in other people's words and worlds. To survive being imperfectly seen. This may itch, but it is not in itself dangerous.

My instinct, always, is to withdraw and invent my own language, my own world. The price of this is never to be visible, never to share the world you live in.

I thank Matt Turner, Hermione Thompson, Athena Bryan, Mike Lindgren, Carl Bromley, and everyone who helped at and beyond Penguin and MelvilleHouse, for helping me make my world shareable.

Those of my family who have not disowned me gave me permission to write this book. Names have been changed to protect everyone. The Leverhulme Trust held an umbrella over me as I wrote, and the AHRC/BBC New Generation Thinkers Scheme gave me a way in. Help and support beyond the call of duty were extended by Rachel Grahame at Newcastle City Council, Nicola at the Orford Ness National Trust Office, and the Ramblers Association (Peterborough Group). Thanks go to Andy Emery and Christopher

Jackson for assistance with Scottish geology and Pasha M. Khan for help with Punjabi (though any mistakes in the book are mine alone), and Lisa, Robert, Judith and Marja, who kindly gave lifts to two awkward strangers on Orkney.

Thank you to Nuzhat Saleem and Farida Chughtai for helping me when I was little. Thank you to Fiona Grace, for her grace.

Thank you, from my heart, to Katie Linden.

I want also to talk about the word 'friend,' and its capaciousness. Historically, in both the East and the West, it's a site of queerness. In Pakistan, you might lie with your friends, you might touch them, you might hold hands in the street: it's not an unerotic mode. In Western letters, 'friend' could be used to cover a gay relationship, or to contain it; to offer space for the whole spectrum of erotic or non-erotic or quasi-erotic ways of relating to other people. 'My friend.' 'My beloved friend.' To me it's a sacred word. My friends keep distance from me as a way of loving me. They accept the way I speak and think. They may not be able to share my world of bones and plants and landscapes—but in this way they hold that world, trustingly, and me within it, busy and alone.

Thank you to Aliyah Norrish, Dan Grausam, Venetia Bridges, Clare Deal, Hannah Ashman, Rakhshan Rizwan, Adam St. Leger-Honeybone, Jacob Lloyd, Millie Schurch, Dave Cook, Robert Sowden, Stephen Blanchard, Peter Riley, Josh Pugh, Tom Cook, Ben Ralph, Emma Cockburn, Ryan Hocking, Sinéad Esler.

This book is for my friends.

References

p. vii   'To say, as some do . . .' Judith Butler, *Giving an Account of Oneself* (New York: Fordham University Press, 2005), p. 65.

Introduction

p. xiii   'If life has a base that it stands upon . . .' Virginia Woolf, 'Sketch of the Past' in *Moments of Being: Autobiographical Writings*, ed. Jeanne Schulkind (London: Pimlico, 2002), pp. 78–160, pp. 78–9.

p. xx   'prolonged, repeated trauma' . . . Judith Lewis Herman, *Trauma and Recovery: From Domestic Abuse to Political Terror* (London: Pandora, 2001), p. 119.

1. The First Flat Place

p. 3   'I see a ring . . .' Virginia Woolf, *The Waves* (Harmondsworth: Penguin, 1964), p. 6.

p. 4   The memory theorist Douwe Draaisma . . . Douwe Draaisma, *Forgetting: Why We Can't Remember Our Dreams, and Other Crucial Quirks of Human Memory*, trans. Liz Waters (New Haven and London: Yale University Press, 2015), p. 27.

p. 21   'If we had a keen vision . . .' George Eliot, *Middlemarch*, ed. David Carroll (Oxford: Oxford University Press, 1997), p. 182.

p. 23   And I thought about the photographs . . . George Didi-Huberman, *Invention of Hysteria: Charcot and the Photographic Iconography of the Salpêtrière*, trans. Alisa Hartz (Cambridge, MA, and London: MIT Press, 2003), p. 113.

p. 27   In *Queer Phenomenology* . . . Sara Ahmed, *Queer Phenomenology: Objects, Orientations, Others* (Durham and London: Duke University Press, 2006), p. 1.

p. 27   Simone Weil wrote . . . Simone Weil, 'Friendship' in *Waiting on God*, trans. Emma Craufurd (London and Glasgow: Fontana, 1959), pp. 152–9, p. 157.

2. From Ely to Welney

p. 29   'We can't be nearly there . . .' Jill Paton Walsh, *Gaffer Samson's Luck* (London: Penguin, 1988), p. 7.

p. 29   **Judith Lewis Herman describes how** . . . Judith Lewis Herman, *Trauma and Recovery: From Domestic Abuse to Political Terror* (London: Pandora, 2001), pp. 42–3.

p. 32   **At twenty, I read an account of this** . . . Amit Chaudhuri, *Clearing a Space: Reflections on India, Literature and Culture* (Oxford: Peter Lang, 2008), pp. 39–56, p. 48.

p. 37   **There's an Old English poem** . . . Anon., 'Wulf and Eadwacer'. Translator of quoted portion unknown; accessed 14 September 2022 at https://pressbooks.pub/earlybritishlit/chapter/exeter-book-elegies-2/.

p. 42   **There are few details** . . . On the stories of Hereward's drunkenness and horse stealing, see Charles Kingsley, *Hereward the Wake* (London: Macmillan and Co., 1898), pp. 18–19; on exile in Ireland, Northumbria and Cornwall, and the fight with a half-human bear, see Peter Rex, *Hereward* (Amberley: Stroud, 2013), pp. 55–8.

p. 43   **When Hereward returned to England** . . . *Gesta Herewardi*, trans. Michael Swanton, accessed 28 September 2022 at https://d.lib.rochester.edu. On the date of the insurrection, Peter Rex puts it around 1069–70. Peter Rex, *Hereward* (Amberley: Stroud, 2013), p. 87.

p. 43   **Hereward infiltrated the Norman camp** . . . *Gesta Herewardi*, trans. Michael Swanton, accessed 28 September 2022 at https://d.lib.rochester.edu.

p. 43   'the [Fenlanders] disdained . . .' Charles Kingsley, *Hereward the Wake* (London: Macmillan and Co., 1898), pp. 3–10.

p. 44   **Does this fantasy** . . . Charles Kingsley, *Hereward the Wake* (London: Macmillan and Co., 1898), p. 19.

p. 44   'Scrafield, Stainfield . . .' Jon McGregor, *This Isn't The Sort Of Thing That Happens To Someone Like You* (London: Bloomsbury, 2012), p. 255.

p. 46   **Well into the seventeenth century** . . . Francis Pryor, *The Fens: Discovering England's Ancient Depths* (London: Head of Zeus, 2019), p. 342.

p. 46   **But the fens are now** . . . Melissa Harrison, *Rain: Four Walks in English Weather* (London: Faber and Faber, 2016), p. 4.

p. 46   **The farmed land** . . . Fens for the Future, accessed 29 September 2022 at https://www.fensforthefuture.org.uk; 'The Breach', accessed 29 September 2022 at https://crowlandbuffalo.wordpress.com.

p. 47   **As sea levels rise** . . . Climate Central, 'Coastal Risk Screening Tool' (2021), accessed 29 September 2022 at https://coastal.climatecentral.org.

p. 50   **The river dates back to the drainage** . . . On the cutting of the New Bedford River, see Norfolk Heritage, 'New Bedford River', accessed 29 September 2022 at https://www.heritage.norfolk.gov.uk; on Vermuyden, see Frank Meeres, 'A Short History of the Fens', The History Press, accessed 29 September 2022 at https://www.thehistorypress.co.uk.

p. 51   **In the seventeenth century** . . . 'A brief history of the Great Fen', Wildlife Trust for Beds, Cambs and Northants, accessed 29 September 2022 at https://www.greatfen.org.uk.

p. 54   **The concept of *nature*** . . . Francis Bacon, *The New Organon*, ed. Lisa Jardine and Michael Silverthorne (Cambridge: Cambridge University Press, 2000), p. 33.

p. 55   **Others, like Rousseau** . . . Jean-Jacques Rousseau, *Rousseau's Émile, or Treatise on Education*, trans. William H. Payne (New York and London: D. Appleton and Company, 1918), p. 1.

p. 57   **Sara Ahmed writes** . . . Sara Ahmed, *The Promise of Happiness* (Durham and London: Duke University Press, 2010), pp. 61–2.

3. Orford Ness, Shingle Street

p. 59   **Its vegetated shingle** . . . On UK vegetated shingle, see 'Coastal Vegetated Shingle' in Ant Maddock, ed. *UK Biodiversity Action Plan; Priority Habitat Descriptions* (BRIG, 2008), accessed 29 September 2022 at https://data.jncc.gov.uk. On vegetated shingle outside the UK, see Buglife, 'Scottish Invertebrate Habitat Management: Coastal Vegetated Shingle' (The Invertebrate Conservation Trust, 2010), p. 1, accessed 29 September 2022 at https://cdn.buglife.org.uk.

p. 60   **Few people visited** . . . National Trust, 'The First World War on Orford Ness', accessed 29 September 2022 at https://www.nationaltrust.org.uk; Paddy Heazell, *Most Secret: The Hidden History of Orford Ness* (Cheltenham: The History Press, 2010), p. 195.

p. 60   **'I imagined myself . . .'** W. G. Sebald, *The Rings of Saturn* (London: Vintage, 2002), p. 237.

p. 68   **The famous red-and-white striped lighthouse** . . . Orfordness Lighthouse Trust, accessed 29 September 2022 at http://www.orfordnesslighthouse.co.uk/.

p. 69   **Back in the 1950s** . . . William Walters, 'Everyday secrecy: Oral history and the social life of a top-secret weapons research establishment during the Cold War', *Security Dialogue*, 51, no. 1 (2020), pp. 60–76.

p. 74 'Alone on the railroad track . . .' Elizabeth Bishop, *The Complete Poems 1927–1979* (London: Hogarth Press, 1984), p. 8.

p. 76 'Now it is September . . .' Wallace Stevens, *Collected Poems* (London: Faber and Faber, 1984), p. 208.

p. 77 The two used to be one country . . . For the basic details, see Ian Talbot, *Pakistan: A Modern History* (London: Palgrave Macmillan, 2005), pp. 186, 188, 195, 212.

p. 82 This seawall had been built by a Chinese labour battalion . . . Xu Guoqi, *Strangers on the Western Front: Chinese Workers in the Great War* (Cambridge, MA: Harvard University Press, 2011).

p. 86 It was made by Lida Kindersley . . . Jeremy Gugenheim, dir. *C Shells*. Outhouse Filmworks, 2017.

p. 86 'Only the whelks, the white whelks . . .' Els Bottema and Lida Lopes Cardozo Kindersley, *The Shingle Street Shell Line* (Cambridge: Cardozo Kindersley, 2018), n. pag.

p. 87 'Of course they're all a bit broken . . .' Jeremy Gugenheim, dir. *C Shells*. Outhouse Filmworks, 2017.

p. 87 Robert Macfarlane . . . Robert Macfarlane and Stanley Donwood, *Ness* (London: Hamish Hamilton, 2019).

p. 88 In Greek drama . . . Oxford English Dictionary, 'catastrophe' and 'cata-' accessed 29 September 2022 at https://www.oed.com.

4. Morecambe Bay

p. 91 'the constant presence . . .' Laura S. Brown, 'Not Outside the Range: One Feminist Perspective on Psychic Trauma', *American Imago* 48, No. 1, 119–33, p. 122.

p. 92 'that unnoticed / & that necessary' . . . Margaret Atwood, 'Variation on the Word *Sleep*' in *Being Alive*, ed. Neil Astley (Tarset: Bloodaxe, 2004), p. 188.

p. 92 The psychoanalyst Robert Stolorow . . . Robert D. Stolorow, *Trauma and Human Existence* (London and New York: Routledge, 2007), p. 16.

p. 93 It's been shown . . . Bessel van der Kolk, *The Body Keeps the Score* (London: Penguin, 2015), pp. 51–2.

p. 93 'Holding them, rocking them . . .' Bessel van der Kolk, 'Trauma and PTSD: Aftermaths of the WTC Disaster—An Interview With Bessel A. van der Kolk, MD', *Medscape*, Oct. 01, 2001, accessed 29 September 2022 at https://www.medscape.com.

p. 93 **The story goes . . .** See Jacqueline Banerjee, 'The Hardy Tree', accessed 29 September 2022 at https://victorianweb.org/photos/hardy/74b.html.

p. 95 **The poet Norman Nicholson . . .** Norman Nicholson, *The Lakers: The Adventures of the First Tourists* (London: Robert Hale Ltd, 1955), p. 76.

p. 96 **For centuries . . .** Guide over Sands Trust, accessed 29 September 2022 at https://www.guideoversands.co.uk/.

p. 98 **Every country is built . . .** On the ambiguities surrounding 'Islam' and 'Muslimness' upon and since Pakistan's foundation, see Farzana Shaikh, *Making Sense of Pakistan* (London: Hurst Press, 2018), pp. 4–5.

p. 101 **In 2004, under the negligent attentions . . .** Press Association, 'The Morecambe Bay Victims, *Guardian*, 24 March 2006, accessed 29 September 2022 at https://www.theguardian.com; 'Man guilty of 21 cockling deaths', *BBC News*, 24 March 2006, accessed 29 September 2022 at http://news.bbc.co.uk; Rachel Ryan, 'Friends swam the wrong way—court hears', *Westmorland Gazette*, 12 October 2005, accessed 29 September 2022 at https://www.thewestmorlandgazette.co.uk.

p. 114 **I remembered reading about the submerged forests . . .** R. D. Irvine, 'Anthropocene East Anglia', *The Sociological Review* 65 (2017), pp. 154–70.

5. Newcastle Moor

p. 117 **'specific lives cannot be apprehended . . .'** Judith Butler, *Frames of War: When is Life Grievable?* (London and New York: Verso, 2009), p. 1.

p. 117 **The green space stretches . . .** Newcastle Local Studies & Family History Centre, 'Town Moor Hoppings' (2009), n. pag.

p. 117 **King John declared . . .** Colin Lofthouse, *Town Moor, Newcastle upon Tyne Archaeological Survey Report* (Newcastle: RCHME, 1995), p. 7.

p. 118 **Since 1774 . . .** Colin Lofthouse, *Town Moor, Newcastle upon Tyne Archaeological Survey Report* (Newcastle: RCHME, 1995), pp. 7, 39, 53; 'Newcastle, Town Moor, Smallpox Hospital Enclosure', accessed 1 October 2022 at https://www.twsitelines.info/smr/5896.

p. 118 **Despite this vigilance . . .** Colin Lofthouse, *Town Moor, Newcastle upon Tyne Archaeological Survey Report* (Newcastle: RCHME, 1995), pp. 12, 20, 22, 24.

p. 118 **In 1861, the Town Moor committee . . .** Rachel Hammersley, 'People's Parks', *Wastes and Strays*, accessed 1 October 2022 at https://research.ncl.ac.uk.

p. 119   **In 1892, a golf course was opened** . . . 'Newcastle, Town Moor Golf Course & Newcastle United Golf Club', accessed 29 September 2022 at https://sitelines.newcastle.gov.uk/SMR/16843; Colin Lofthouse, *Town Moor, Newcastle upon Tyne Archaeological Survey Report* (Newcastle: RCHME, 1995), p. 10.

p. 119   **Something like the wood between the worlds** . . . C. S. Lewis, *The Magician's Nephew* (London: HarperCollins, 2001), pp. 39–40.

p. 119   **'Our aim will be to keep . . .'** Siouxsie Wiles, 'The three phases of Covid-19—and how we can make it manageable', *The Spinoff*, 9 March 2020, accessed 29 September 2022 at https://thespinoff.co.nz.

p. 131   **In 2003, I learned** . . . 'Moor is named wasted space', *Chronicle Live*, 27 September 2003, accessed 29 September 2022 at https://www.chroniclelive.co.uk.

p. 132   **After digging around online** . . . Colin Lofthouse, *Town Moor, Newcastle upon Tyne Archaeological Survey Report* (Newcastle: RCHME, 1995), p. 12.

p. 132   **As I worked my way** . . . Colin Lofthouse, *Town Moor, Newcastle upon Tyne Archaeological Survey Report* (Newcastle: RCHME, 1995), p. 17.

p. 133   **In fact, I discovered, an MP protested** . . . Shapurji Dorabji Saklatvala, transcribed in *North-East Coast Exhibition (African Village)—Hansard—UK Parliament. Volume 227: debated on Wednesday 8 May 1929*, accessed 14 September 2022 at https://hansard.parliament.uk.

6. Orkney

p. 147   **Both are expected to offer** . . . John Bowlby, *A Secure Base* (London and New York: Routledge, 2005), see especially p. 13.

p. 157   **Most of the flat landscapes I'd visited** . . . Alan McKirdy, *Orkney and Shetland: A Landscape Fashioned By Geology* (Perth: Scottish National Heritage, 2010), pp. 2, 14–15.

p. 158   **This is one creation story** . . . Tom Muir, *Orkney Folk Tales* (Cheltenham: The History Press, 2014), e-book, n.pag.

p. 164   **Norse mythology is full of tales** . . . Rachel Pickering, 'The Giants of Orkney', accessed 1 October 2022 at https://www.historicenvironment.scot; 'Orkney's Giant Folklore', *Orkneyjar*, accessed at http://www.orkneyjar.com.

p. 165   **The Stones of Stenness** . . . 'Stones of Stenness Circle and Henge', *Historic Scotland*, accessed 1 October 2022 at https://www.historicenvironment.scot.

p. 166   **The archaeologist Colin Richards** . . . Colin Richards, 'Rethinking the Great Stone Circles of Northwest Britain', *Papers and Pictures in*

Honour of Daphne Home Lorimer MBE (Orkney Archaeological Trust, 2004), accessed 1 October 2022 at https://www.orkneyjar.com.

p. 172   **Despite its general flatness . . .** Tom Muir, *Orkney Folk Tales* (Cheltenham: The History Press, 2014), e-book, n.pag.

The Way Home

p. 189   **'What worth are your small sufferings . . .'** Sanam Marvi, 'Yaar Vekho', Coke Studio, Season 6, 2013, accessed 29 September 2022 at https://www.youtube.com.

p. 190   **'On each patch of green . . .'** Faiz Ahmed Faiz, 'City of Lights' in *The Rebel's Silhouette: Selected Poems*, trans. Agha Shahid Ali (Amherst: The University of Massachusetts Press, 1995), pp. 32–3.

p. 190   **Faiz, a Communist . . .** 'About Faiz Ahmed Faiz', *poets.org*, accessed 1 October 2022 at https://poets.org/poet/faiz-ahmed-faiz.

p. 191   **This is a jab . . .** Abigail Beall, 'Abdus Salam: The Muslim science genius forgotten by history', *BBC News*, 15 October 2019, accessed 1 October 2022 at https://www.bbc.com.

p. 205   **When it was an empire . . .** 'The Fabric of India: Textiles in a Changing World', *Victoria & Albert Museum*, accessed 1 October 2022 at http://www.vam.ac.uk; Ibtisam Ahmed, 'The British Empire's homophobic legacy could finally be overturned in India', 1 September 2017, accessed 1 October 2022 at https://theconversation.com.

p. 205   **And then, when Cyril Radcliffe . . .** Pippa Virdee, *From the Ashes of 1947: Reimagining Punjab* (Cambridge: Cambridge University Press, 2018), p. 55.

p. 210   **Donald Winnicott thought . . .** See Donald Winnicott, 'The Theory of the Parent-Infant Relationship', in *The Maturational Processes and the Facilitating Environment* (London: Hogarth, 1965), pp. 37–35, p. 47.

About the Author

Born in Pakistan, Noreen Masud is a lecturer in twentieth-century literature at the University of Bristol in the United Kingdom. In 2020, she was named as one of the BBC Radio 3 and the Arts and Humanities Research Council's 10 New Generation Thinkers.